BLACK BIRDS IN THE SKY

ALSO BY BRANDY COLBERT

The Voting Booth

The Only Black Girls in Town

The Revolution of Birdie Randolph

Finding Yvonne

Little & Lion

Pointe

BLACK BIRDS IN THE SKY

THE STORY AND LEGACY OF THE 1921 TULSA RACE MASSACRE

BRANDY COLBERT

BALZER + BRAY
An Imprint of HarperCollins*Publishers*

Balzer + Bray is an imprint of HarperCollins Publishers.

Black Birds in the Sky
Copyright © 2021 by Brandy Colbert

ISBN 978-0-06-305666-4

Typography by Michelle Gengaro-Kokmen
21 22 23 24 25 PC/LSCH 10 9 8 7 6 5 4 3 2 1
❖
First Edition

For the victims and survivors of the Tulsa Race Massacre of 1921
and
the Greenwood District

CONTENTS

Foreword 1

May 30, 1921 13

1: Oklahoma! Soon Be Livin' in a
Brand-New State 19

2: To Be Black in America 43

3: Fighting for Survival 69

May 31, 1921 91

4: Black Wall Street Comes Alive 103

5: Extra! Extra! Read All About It!, or
the Promise of a Lynching 119

June 1, 1921 135

6: The Aftermath 153

7: The Legacy of Greenwood 167

Afterword 189

Acknowledgments 205

Source List and Images Credits 207

Index 215

Foreword

By the time I'd reached fourth grade, the lesson I dreaded most was our history unit on slavery.

I attended a predominantly white school in a predominantly white Missouri town, and more often than not, I felt like I fit in well enough. Some people went out of their way to point out my differences, like my highly textured hair that would curl and thicken at the scalp when my chemical relaxer started to grow out. Or they'd hold their arm up to mine when they'd gotten a particularly good tan, showing me that they were "almost as dark" as me. There were other microaggressions, of course— way too many to name here. It was southwest Missouri, and it was the 1980s. Racial sensitivity wasn't high on most people's list of priorities.

History class felt uninspired and repetitive for much of the year, but the few days we spent learning about Black Americans were excruciating. I was embarrassed when our teachers talked about the African people who'd been stolen from their continent and brought to the United States to be part of a chattel slavery system; I didn't like the way both the teachers and the textbooks talked about enslaved people as if they weren't actual human beings with hopes and dreams and emotions and profound mental strength. I also didn't like that heads automatically swiveled to find me, to see how I was reacting to the lesson because I was one of the only Black people they'd ever met in their entire lives.

And, in retrospect, I hated that the room was uncomfortably silent during the lesson; that nobody asked why we never learned about anyone apart from basic biographies of Frederick Douglass and Harriet Tubman; that no actual countries in Africa were ever named, which is likely why so many Americans still think Africa is a country rather than a continent; and that the lesson never explicitly stated how much the violent, genocidal foundation of this country shaped everything about how our nation operates today.

Perhaps the most insulting part about the units covering centuries of Black history is that they were so brief—we spent maybe a week on the topic, if that. Reconstruction was never explained in a meaningful way. The civil rights lesson was, again, focused on sanitized versions of two people: Rosa Parks and Dr. Martin Luther King Jr. I never came across the names of voting rights activists Fannie Lou Hamer or Stokely Carmichael or John Lewis in our textbooks. And I can't remember one mention of Shirley Chisholm, the first Black woman elected to Congress, as well as the first woman *and* Black woman to run for a major political party's nomination for president of the United States.

The fact that there was no separate, detailed lesson about the Trail of Tears, which ran *right through our hometown*, was particularly egregious.

I blame the history texts more than my individual teachers. For the most part, I know the curriculum was not up to them. And I know that some of them, all white women and men, were inherently uncomfortable teaching lessons about such traumatic times in our country's history. But all these years later, after meeting so many dedicated, progressive, and passionate educators around the country, I have to wonder: Why didn't just one of my teachers care enough to go off script? To sit in their discomfort so we could have honest conversations about our past? To not only challenge us to learn more but to challenge themselves as well?

When you are a Black person from Missouri, most people assume you grew up in St. Louis, which is nearly 50 percent Black. Or maybe Kansas City, with a population that's just under 30 percent African American. I've shocked many people when I tell them that I'm from Springfield, the third-largest city in the state, whose nickname is the Queen City of the Ozarks. (*City* is a generous word. When I was growing up, Springfield felt more like a big town, and even in 2019, the population was just over 167,000.) Springfield was about 3 percent Black during my childhood and teenage years, in the 1980s and '90s, and the demographics haven't changed much since then. I didn't know about percentages when I was younger, but I did know that besides the Black church my family and I attended each week, I seldom saw other Black people outside my home.

Just a few weeks after I started second grade, my parents moved my brother and me to the south side of town, which was almost exclusively white. I'll never forget walking into my new classroom; every set of eyes that stared back at me came from a white face. The principal was white, my teachers were white, and for the majority of my time in elementary school, I was the only Black girl in my class. Junior high seemed a bit more promising; there were, at least, a handful of Black kids in my seventh-grade class. But people moved away or went to different schools, and that number didn't increase by much in high school.

It never occurred to me to wonder *why* the town was so white. It just was. But the older I got, I did start to wonder why my parents had chosen to live there. Sure, Springfield was affordable. They'd bought their first house together there, renovated part of it, and then bought their second home when I was seven years old. But why Springfield in particular?

My parents, who once would have been described as Black people who "pulled themselves up by their bootstraps," had grown up in Jim Crow Arkansas, thirty minutes from the town of Elaine, which, according to the *New York Times*, suffered "one of the worst episodes of racial violence in American history," in 1919. (My mother recently told me that some of our ancestors migrated from Elaine in the decades following the massacre to the town where she grew up, and I have to wonder if they had been there to see the destruction and violence that took over their town.) My mom and dad grew up in poor farming families; they worked from a young age picking cotton in their parents' fields and shared beds with their many siblings. My mother is one of thirteen kids, my father one of ten.

I was in my twenties before I really comprehended my parents' origin story in the Ozarks. I learned that, after a brief stint in Louisville, Kentucky, my father's job at an electronics company transferred him to Springfield, Missouri, in the early 1970s. And that, once they arrived, they had so much trouble renting an apartment that my father had to ask his white supervisor to cosign the rental application—not because they were so young, but because they were Black. Fifteen years later, when they moved us to the white side of town, we were the first Black family to integrate our solidly middle-class street.

We traveled by car more often than plane, and when we did fly, it was usually out of the tiny airport in Springfield. But, if the price was right, we'd drive the three hours north to fly out of St. Louis or Kansas City. And, sometimes, we'd travel three hours southwest to fly out of Tulsa, Oklahoma.

I don't remember much about the Tulsa of my childhood; I probably didn't see much more than airport terminals, restaurants, and hotels. But when I drove cross-country to and from Los Angeles—twice in my twenties and once in my thirties—I never minded stopping in Oklahoma. Tulsa was a town where, as a young Black woman traveling alone, I was unafraid to stop for snacks or to fill up my gas tank, especially compared to the long line of conservative areas I had to travel through on that route.

Tulsa reminded me of my hometown: primarily white, and not necessarily an ideal place for a Black person to live, but it felt safe. I remember that, when I was a child, my parents had even considered moving to a town just fifty miles from Tulsa, when my father was being courted by an oil company. So it couldn't be worse than Springfield, right?

It wasn't until I was living in Los Angeles that I first read about the 1906 triple lynching in Springfield. Although the complex history of lynching hadn't been discussed in my history classes, either, I was well aware that it was a form of vigilante justice that had historically been used to intimidate and ultimately kill Black people, typically by hanging. On the one hundredth anniversary, my hometown newspaper, the *Springfield News-Leader*, ran a series of articles about the three murdered Black men: Horace B. Duncan, Fred Coker, and Will Allen. Duncan and Coker, coworkers and lifelong friends, had been falsely accused of assault and rape by a white couple and arrested. Once their white employer provided alibis, explaining they'd been at work at the time of the crime, they were set free.

But later that same evening, the white man who'd claimed they assaulted him now accused Duncan of stealing his watch. Both Duncan and Coker were arrested again, and this time, the people of Springfield decided they didn't need to know the truth before they sought their own justice. A mob of up to a thousand white people dragged the two young men from the city jail, hanged them from Gottfried Tower in the center of the public square, and burned their bodies in a fire at the base of the tower. By the end of the violent display, the overall crowd at the square is estimated to have totaled around three thousand people.

But they weren't done. Drunk with power and high on violence, the mob returned to the city jail, where they found Will Allen—a Black man accused of murdering a white man—still locked in his cell. It wasn't long before he, too, was removed from the jail, given a mock trial, and lynched in the same spot as Coker and Duncan.

The *News-Leader* reported that Mayor-Elect James Blain climbed the tower and told the lynch mob: "Men, you have done enough. You have had your revenge. You [had] better go home." They finally did, but not before they took pieces of rope, clothing, and bone to remember their gleeful lynching.

The next morning was Easter Sunday.

Before the lynching, about 2,300 Black people lived in Springfield, roughly 10 percent of the town's population. Black Springfieldians were city leaders, doctors, preachers, lawyers, teachers, and skilled tradesmen. They sat on the city council and the school board, held jobs in law enforcement, and owned popular and successful businesses. The largest grocery store in Springfield, Hardrick Bros., was owned by a Black family and carried several specialty items that were impossible to find at other stores in the area. And Walter Majors, a Black man who repaired violins and worked as a bicycle mechanic, built and owned one of the rare horseless buggies in town.

But the lynchings changed everything. Martial law was declared afterward, and a grand jury convened, eventually finding Duncan and Coker "not guilty of assault." The jury's report went on to say that the sheriff had acted accordingly to stop the mob violence, but the jury condemned the police department, which "seemed to have no appreciation of their duties and responsibilities as officers of the law." And although nearly twenty men were indicted for the lynchings—including a former policeman and individuals associated with the police department—all charges were eventually dropped. This was a clear sign of how Springfield felt about its Black residents—as well as how such racist violence would be handled in the future. The Black community recognized this and left town in droves.

The morning after the lynchings, the *News-Leader* reported that while white people visited the lynching site on their way to and from church "dressed in Easter finery," Black Springfield-ians "were scarce on public streets." Some still attended church to observe the holiday, but the train station saw record numbers of Black people heading out of town, while others fled in horse-drawn wagons. Those who didn't have access or means to transportation left on foot. About half the Black popula-tion departed in the years following the tragedy; the number declined even more in the following decades.

Like the massacre that would take place in Tulsa fifteen years later, the lynchings in Springfield were spurred by racial tension that had been growing for some time. In 1901, two Black men were arrested for the murder of a white woman in Pierce City, a town fifty miles west of Springfield, by the Okla-homa border; one of the men, William Godley, was lynched. After a mob burned and terrorized the Black neighborhood, the nearly three hundred Black people who lived in Pierce City left within a day, never returning to their home. In 1903, the Black community of Joplin, another small city in southwest Missouri, was forced out of town when a young Black man named Thomas Gilyard was accused of killing a white police officer and lynched by a mob before any sort of trial could take place.

And Springfield, which had previously served as a refuge for Black people who felt unsafe in nearby towns, began to show signs of the same type of racial intolerance shortly before the three lynchings. In 1904, a Black man rumored to be the biological father of a married white woman's mixed-race child was arrested for attempted assault and burglary. He was eventually sentenced to thirty years in prison but only narrowly avoided being lynched by the woman's husband—a police officer—and hundreds of other white men. The sheriff, sensing there would be an attempt at vigilante justice, had moved him to the jail in the next county over. (The woman's husband, Jesse Brake, was the former policeman indicted in the 1906 lynchings just two years later.) In December 1905, two Black men were arrested—likely with little to no evidence—as suspects in the murder of a local white man. And just a month later, in January 1906, two Black men were similarly arrested for the murder of a white Civil War veteran.

For many years, no one talked about this violence or its long-term effects on the racial diversity of the region. It had been news to me, and I'd been born and raised there, living in Springfield for twenty-two years. But once people learned about their history, they began to speak up, to seek truth and justice for these unpunished crimes.

In August 2002, amid controversy, the city of Springfield erected a bronze plaque in the square that reads:

ON APRIL 14, 1906, THREE BLACK MEN,
HORACE B. DUNCAN, FRED COKER
AND WILL ALLEN
WERE LYNCHED WITHOUT A TRIAL

I visited the plaque in 2018. It is small—just four inches by twelve inches—and difficult to find, even when you are looking for it. I didn't know it at the time, but 2018 was the same year that Joplin residents memorialized lynching victim Gilyard, with plans to send a jar of soil to the National Memorial for Peace and Justice in Montgomery, Alabama, which acknowledges victims of racial injustice from the nation's past.

A year later, in October 2019, a large crowd gathered in my hometown's square once again, this time to celebrate the dedication of a new historical marker commemorating Duncan, Coker, and Allen. Set on a pedestal, the marker is large, bold, and easy to find.

This history is painful. It angers me. It hurts to see just how many ways my life and my ancestors' lives have been affected by white supremacy. But I am grateful for historians, social justice activists, and politicians who have made it their mission to ensure this history will no longer be buried. I am grateful for educators who continue to do the difficult work of teaching their students the complicated, sometimes brutal history of this country's past. Because, as I have learned, the fight to remember and acknowledge the shameful parts of our past is just as challenging as many other components of the battle for racial justice.

I still have so much to learn, especially when it comes to Black history. But I no longer dread learning about it. Because, now, I'm not limited to studying one subject over the course of a few days. I can learn about the beautiful parts of my ancestors' lives, along with the pain they had to endure. And I know that the more I can learn and share with others, the better off I— and hopefully they—will be.

The Tulsa Race Massacre was a shameful, completely preventable tragedy, like so many incidents in United States history. But the Greenwood District is proof that Black people have always been willing to work hard, to make the best out of unequal treatment and unjust laws, and to thrive in our community when others won't let us into theirs. And the legacy of Black Wall Street is one that endures, even one hundred years after its destruction.

It is a privilege to continue telling the stories like those from my hometown and Tulsa so that they cannot be forgotten.

I saw what I thought were little black birds dropping out of the sky over the Greenwood District. But those were no little birds; what was falling from the sky over the Negro District, as it was called in those days, were bullets and devices to set fires, and debris of all kinds.

—Genevieve Elizabeth Tillman Jackson,
Tulsa Race Massacre survivor

May 30, 1921

Memorial Day 1921 began just like any other in Tulsa, Oklahoma, with many shops and stores closed for business as townspeople prepared for the big parade that would proceed down Main Street that morning. But one business that remained open on the busy street was a shoeshine parlor that employed a nineteen-year-old Black man named Dick Rowland.

Rowland had lived a rough life in his two short decades. His birthplace is unknown, but he was born Jimmie Jones, and had two older sisters. By 1908, the three siblings were living as orphans on the streets of Vinita, Oklahoma, a town about sixty-five miles northeast of present-day Tulsa. Forced to seek shelter in the woods and under bridges, Jimmie and his sisters regularly begged for food to survive.

This was how he met a young, divorced Black woman named Damie Ford, who operated a small grocery store and lived alone. After feeding Jimmie a meal and listening to his proposition to help her around the business in exchange for food, Ford checked with Jimmie's sisters to make sure it was okay if she took in Jimmie, who appeared to be about six years old. They readily agreed, as that would be one less person they'd have to worry about in their hard-luck family.

Jimmie, who called his adopted mother Aunt Dame, quickly made himself useful, shelving products and cleaning the one-room grocery store and endearing himself to Ford's customers. However, though Ford was generous in spirit and made sure Jimmie was clothed, fed, and housed, the store didn't bring in a lot of money, and she struggled to support the two of them. About a year after Jimmie came to live with her, they moved to Tulsa, where he met Ford's family, the Rowlands, and where Ford hoped for more opportunities in the booming oil town.

Ford moved to the Greenwood District, a thriving Black community in Tulsa across the train tracks from where most of the white homes and businesses were located. At the time, Oklahoma was still heavily enforcing Jim Crow laws: mandates that segregated Black Americans from white Americans. This included housing, and because Black people were often banned from moving into white neighborhoods, they created their own district. Greenwood was founded in 1906, when a Black businessman named O. W. Gurley purchased forty acres of land to establish an all-Black residential and business district.

The landmark 1896 US Supreme Court case *Plessy v.*

Ferguson, which established the legality of Jim Crow legislation, stated spaces and accommodations segregated by race were legal as long as they were comparable; this is where the standard of "separate but equal" was born. The "equal" part rarely came to fruition with Black spaces and accommodations; Greenwood, however, was something of an anomaly in this respect. By 1914, the neighborhood boasted all kinds of Black professionals, from doctors and lawyers to business owners, educators, and newspaper publishers—and they kept their wealth within the community, continually supporting the businesses of what became known nationwide as Black Wall Street.

After moving to Greenwood, Damie Ford initially worked various jobs to make ends meet, eventually buying her own home on Archer Street. She rented out rooms to tenants to bring in money; Jimmie cleaned these rooms and also took on odd jobs to help out with expenses.

Maybe it was the change in location, or maybe it was getting to know his adopted family, but Jimmie soon took on a new name. His first day in elementary school, he introduced himself as Dick Rowland, and at home, he asked that Aunt Dame use that name for him, too. As a young kid, Rowland was a good student, but his interest in academics waned the older he got. By the time he was a teenager, he was known more for high school football—he would drop out of school at times when the football season was finished—and his participation in Greenwood's nightlife scene.

Rowland began ditching classes at Booker T. Washington High School to take a job shining shoes at a white-owned establishment in downtown Tulsa. He made a decent amount of money at the shoeshine parlor with generous tips from its white clientele and so found no reason to get his high school diploma and work toward a higher-paying, higher-status job, as Aunt Dame encouraged him to do.

On Memorial Day 1921, Rowland found himself in the Drexel Building on Main Street, where he had to go to use the restroom, as there were no "colored" bathrooms in the shoeshine parlor. Back then, elevators required manual operation to run up and down the floors of buildings, and the elevator operator that day was a young white woman named Sarah Page. While little is known about Rowland's life, even less seems to be known about Page. She had supposedly already been married and divorced by the time she was seventeen, in 1921, and had moved to Tulsa from Kansas City, Missouri, to start over, renting a room in a boardinghouse on North Boston Avenue.

It is rumored that Rowland and Page had known each other prior to that Memorial Day, which would make sense, as Rowland had to visit the Drexel Building to use the facilities during his work shifts and would likely run into Page sometimes. But it was also said by some, including Rowland's Aunt Dame, that they had, perhaps, been romantically involved—and one of the biggest taboos in early-twentieth-century America was a relationship between a Black man and a white woman. Black men were routinely met with threats, violence, and murder for dating white women. In fact, the majority of lynchings that occurred at the time were of Black men arrested for unproven accusations of raping white women—some of which were cover-ups for situations in which white women were caught in consensual relationships with them.

Few details have been confirmed about what happened in that elevator on May 30, 1921—Rowland and Page may be the only ones who actually knew. But what is known for sure is that Rowland used the elevator that day, which Page was operating. The police later determined that Rowland tripped while entering the elevator, reached out, and caught Page's arm for balance, causing her to scream out in surprise. A salesclerk from Renberg's clothing store on the first floor of the building heard the scream, saw Rowland hurrying out of the building, and called the police, assuming Page had been the victim of an attempted rape.

There are no records of what Page told the police, but the damage was already done by the time they spoke to her and the Renberg's clerk. They had a description of an alleged assailant.

Dick Rowland was a wanted man.

That was the saddest day of my life. That riot cheated us out of childhood innocence. My life dreams were destroyed too by that riot.

—Beulah Lane Keenan Smith,
Tulsa Race Massacre survivor

Oklahoma! Soon Be Livin' in a Brand-New State

What comes to mind when you think of Oklahoma? Perhaps one of the thirty-nine Native Nations who call the state home, such as the Cherokee Nation, or Muscogee (Creek) Nation. Or maybe it's the classic Rodgers and Hammerstein musical *Oklahoma!*, which was first performed onstage nearly eighty years ago. Some people simply refer to it as part of "flyover country," one of the large, blocky states between the coasts that many travelers don't encounter unless they're setting off on a cross-country road trip.

Life in Oklahoma may not be as familiar to people living in other parts of the country, but its history is as rich and complicated as the rest of the United States. In 1907, Oklahoma became the forty-sixth state admitted to the Union, although the land first became part of the United States in 1803 as part of the Louisiana Purchase: a deal the young nation had brokered with France to purchase nearly 830,000 square miles of land in North America between the Rocky Mountains and the Mississippi River. French military dictator Napoleon Bonaparte had acquired the Louisiana Territory from Spain in 1800—with plans to use the land as a granary for his proposed sugar empire—and this had made Americans nervous; the French, who were more powerful, now controlled New Orleans, which was significant because it served as a port for Americans to trade goods. So, at the request of President Thomas Jefferson and with the help of US minister to France Robert Livingston, founding father James Monroe sailed overseas to France and eventually purchased the land for $15 million.

However, the land that would become Oklahoma had been settled by Indigenous people centuries before the Louisiana Purchase.

Crossing into the state from the Texas border, travelers are greeted by a sign that reads:

WELCOME TO OKLAHOMA: NATIVE AMERICAN COUNTRY

Today, Indigenous people and Alaska Natives comprise 17.4 percent of Oklahoma's population—second only to Alaska, where Indigenous people encompass 27.9 percent of the population. But how did nearly forty Native Nations come to call the area home?

The Clovis and Folsom cultures, known as Big Game hunters capable of taking on mammoths, mastodons, and massive giant bison, lived in the area as early as 9500 BCE. They also collected a wide variety of plants and engaged in trade networks that brought goods from great distances. This period was followed by the Archaic, where for the next six thousand years, people lived by collecting and gathering, with supplemental hunting. Later, Southern Plains Villagers lived in the central region, building villages near water so they could utilize the farmland, growing food such as beans, corn, and squash. They were successful at working with their hands in a variety of ways, creating pottery and tools made from bone. By the 1500s, these Indigenous groups suffered large population losses, decimated by violent European colonizers and the diseases those invaders brought with them. Spanish explorer Francisco Vázquez de Coronado first set foot in present-day Oklahoma in 1541 and eventually claimed the land, even though several Native Nations lived there. Explorers from France then arrived in the early 1700s, beginning a decades-long struggle for power with Spain over land that belonged to neither one of the countries— a struggle that continued until the United States acquired the land in the Louisiana Purchase.

One of the United States' most shameful and disruptive periods in history occurred twenty-seven years after this land was purchased, when Congress passed the Indian Removal Act in 1830. The act was signed into law by President Andrew Jackson—whose face you may know from the earliest versions of the twenty-dollar bill and who was himself no stranger to cruelty. Jackson was born into poverty but grew his wealth through slave labor: he enslaved about 150 people, some of whom were forced to serve him even during his tenure at the White House. Jackson was a violent man, brutally whipping his enslaved workers in public and promising extra lashes to runaways who were captured. As president, he worked hard to uphold the institution of slavery, opposing laws that would prohibit holding enslaved people in the rapidly expanding western territories.

However, Jackson is perhaps better known for his vicious treatment of Indigenous people. The Indian Removal Act would force nearly fifty thousand Indigenous people to leave their homes and relocate to unsettled land in the West so that their more desirable land east of the Mississippi could be given to white people. These millions of acres in southern states like Florida, Alabama, Tennessee, and Georgia—which had been owned and cared for by Indigenous people for several generations— were prime areas for growing cotton, one of the most prosperous crops for plantation owners. White people also wanted access to Cherokee land in northern Georgia to mine for gold.

Even considering America's long history of anti-Native behavior and policies, the Indian Removal Act was notable in its unfairness and cruelty. Similar to the enslaved people he forced to work for him, Jackson didn't see Indigenous people as fully human, much less American; he believed they were uncivilized simply because they had different ways of life than white people, and he referred to them with paternalistic ethnic slurs to justify his anti-Native views. Dating back to the nation's first president, George Washington, many colonists called the mere existence of Indigenous people "the Indian problem" and continuously worked to strip them of their customs and land. In some cases, white elected officials and church leaders actively pursued policies that would have the citizens of Native Nations abandon their own languages and spiritual beliefs, and even encouraged them to purchase enslaved Africans for labor.

The Five Tribes of Oklahoma

The Five Tribes of Oklahoma, previously referred to as the Five Civilized Tribes, hail from the southeastern United States and include the Cherokee, Chickasaw, Choctaw, Muscogee (Creek), and Seminole Nations. The federal government forcibly removed all of these Native Nations to what is now the eastern half of Oklahoma, but was then called Indian Territory.

The term *Five Civilized Tribes* was primarily assigned to these Native Nations because of their perceived assimilation into white US culture. Many of them spoke English, practiced the Christian religion, drew up written constitutions, married whites, and enslaved African people. *Civilized* was a term that also served to foster division within these Native Nations among their citizens, who had a variety of lifestyles, including those that held more closely to traditional ways. While some leaders within these Native Nations saw adopting parts of Anglo customs as necessary to avoid removal and stop the encroachment of whites taking their land, they were mistaken.

As president, Jackson signed nearly seventy individual removal treaties with Native Nations, which ultimately bullied them into trading the land they and their ancestors had cultivated for a new life on reservations in Indian Territory, including those in what is now Oklahoma. Not all the tribes agreed with these treaties. Some of them were signed by smaller groups within larger bands or tribes that did not believe they should give up their home. And although some outright refused to relocate, they were all eventually forced off the land by the US military, in violation of the law, which required the government to negotiate the removals "fairly, voluntarily, and peacefully."

The Choctaw Nation, who lived in present-day Mississippi, Alabama, Louisiana, and Florida, were the first to be removed, in 1831—and they were forced to travel to the unfamiliar territory on foot. Not only were they made to walk hundreds of miles, but they didn't receive any food or supplies from the very government that had forced them off their land. Thousands of Choctaw people died on this unnecessary journey. Five years later, the US government forced the Muscogee (Creek) from their land, who also lost thousands of their people.

Like other Native Nations, the Cherokee people did not want to leave their homeland—and they used several methods to resist. They sent young representatives around the country to speak out on the issue; circulated a petition that garnered thousands of signatures of Cherokee people protesting the removal; started a newspaper to broadcast their opinions; and tried to appeal to Congress, even going as far as the US Supreme Court, which ruled in their favor. However, President Jackson didn't always follow the law when it worked against him, and he dodged the decision by enforcing yet another treaty. So beginning in the fall of 1838 and lasting through winter 1839, the Cherokee people were removed from their land in Georgia, imprisoned in "roundup camps," and forced to walk over a thousand miles to their new home in Oklahoma. More than four thousand Cherokee people died along the way, with about half of the deaths occurring in the camps due to unsanitary conditions, and the rest during their routes along land and water.

A Choctaw leader called this brutal and often deadly migration that forced Indigenous people from their land "a trail of tears and death," and it has been known as the Trail of Tears ever since. The National Park Service has commemorated the plight of the Cherokee people with the Trail of Tears National Historic Trail, which encompasses 5,043 miles across nine states.

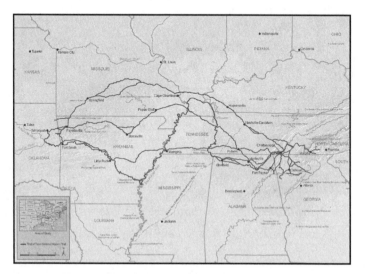

The National Park Service's Trail of Tears National Historic Trail commemorates the routes traveled by the Cherokee people after their forced removal from their ancestral homelands.

Tulsa was first settled by the Muscogee (Creek) Nation in the 1830s, after their forced migration from the South. The Lower Muscogee (Creek) people settled in present-day Tulsa in 1833, then entered into a treaty with the US government that negotiated boundaries between their tribe and the Cherokee Nation in what was then known as Indian Territory. Upper Muscogee (Creek) citizens from the town of Loachapoka, Alabama, made their way along the Trail of Tears with ashes from the final fires in their homeland. When they arrived at the end of the trail in 1836, they spread the ashes over the place that would become their new home. The Muscogee (Creek) Nation built their new locations by several rivers, including the Arkansas River. This particular site would eventually become Cheyenne Avenue, not far from where the Greenwood District would one day be established. The Council Oak Tree is a historic landmark that denotes the site where the Muscogee (Creek) citizens settled, marking present-day Tulsa. The Muscogee (Creek) Nation holds an annual Council Oak Ceremony at Creek Nation Council Oak Park to "celebrate the Mvskoke (Muscogee) people and reflect on the tribe's history and triumphs over the years."

So how did Tulsa get its name? Like those of many cities and towns in the United States, its name was derived from an Indigenous language. According to some historians, *Tulsa* comes from the word *Tullahassee*, which was a Muscogee (Creek) town in present-day Alabama. Still, others believe it was derived from the Mvskoke word *Tallasi*, a shortened version of *Tullahassee* or *Tallahassee*, which means "old town."

Tulsa was incorporated in 1898, but one of its most important families, the Perrymans, first settled there seventy years earlier. Benjamin Perryman, whose mother was a Muscogee (Creek) woman and whose father was thought to be a white Englishman, relocated to Indian Territory in 1828, beginning his family's long history in the city now known as Tulsa. Benjamin's Muscogee name was Steek-cha-ko-me-co, meaning "great king." He settled into his new home with his family, which included eight children.

The Perryman family would come to manage thousands of cattle on the more than 200,000 acres they owned. According to a 1937 issue of the *Chronicles of Oklahoma*, Benjamin's grandson George was known as the "Indian cattle king of the Creek Nation." Another grandson, Josiah, was the first postmaster of Tulsa, and his brother Legus was principal chief of the Muscogee (Creek) Nation for several years.

The family tree is diverse with many branches, as in addition to marrying within the Muscogee (Creek) Nation, some Perrymans married interracially, and some of the Africans they enslaved also took the Perryman name. The Tulsa area is still home to many of the family's descendants, and a significant portion of the city sits on what was once Perryman land.

Land has always been a fundamental issue in the United States. This was, perhaps, never truer in Oklahoma than in the late 1800s, also known as the era of land runs. White settlers had previously seen Oklahoma as undesirable land, which was one of the reasons the government chose it for relocation of the Native Nations forced from their homelands in the first half of the nineteenth century. But by the end of the 1800s, as the country continued to grow and expand west, people found better methods for tending to land and animals—and white colonizers turned their eyes to Oklahoma and the surrounding areas.

In 1887, the Dawes Act—also known as the General Allotment Act—was passed by Congress, which allowed the federal government to parcel out tribal lands into individual plots. This legislation was supposedly passed to protect the property of Native Nations, but, in effect, it divided up communally held tribal lands, allowing "surplus" lands to be claimed by white settlers and railroad companies.

And then, caving to pressure, President Benjamin Harrison made a decision that would once again cheat Indigenous people out of what they owned. Initially, he opened up for settlement nearly two million acres that had not been designated to any specific tribe, but it wasn't long before he permitted white settlers to claim sections that had been assigned to Indigenous people.

In March 1889, President Harrison announced that 1.9 million acres of Indian Territory would be ready for the taking at noon sharp on April 22. People traveled from all over the United States to lay claim to the land, and per the Homestead Act of 1862, passed during the American Civil War, anyone who remained on the land for five years, had "never borne arms against the United States government," and "improved" the land would be the owner. People who participated in the land run were called Boomers, and they didn't waste time preparing for April 22. (Sooners, which you may know as the nickname of the state and mascot of the University of Oklahoma, was the name assigned to people who illegally staked their claim before the official noon start time.) Thousands of people began congregating around the borders of the territory, erecting tent cities on all sides. Hopeful Boomers arrived on horseback, in covered wagons, and even by foot.

By the time April 22 rolled around, more than fifty thousand people were ready and waiting for the ceremonious gunshots, booming cannons, and blaring horns that would signify the land run had officially begun. And by day's end, tens of thousands of people had laid down roots in the territory, forming towns such as Oklahoma City and Norman.

Oklahoma hosted seven land runs in all, from the first one in 1889 to the last in 1895, which took place on land previously designated to the Kickapoo Tribe. Throughout these six years and seven events, the government implemented a lottery system to assign the claims.

Luck, along with white supremacy, was on the side of the colonizers. They'd acquired land that was never meant to be theirs—and it would prove even more valuable than they could have imagined.

Kentucky Daisey and the
Women of the Oklahoma Land Runs

Though women weren't afforded many rights and opportunities at the time, nothing stood in the way of their participation in Oklahoma's land runs. The Homestead Act of 1862 allowed for single women who were head of their household to claim 160 acres. And hundreds of these women—some widowed, some Black—took full advantage.

Perhaps the most famous is the outspoken Nanitta Daisey, also known as "Kentucky Daisey," who'd already made a name for herself in her home state as a newspaper reporter and an educator. Oklahoma legend has it that Daisey, on assignment to cover the first land run in 1889, leaped off a moving train to stake her claim to land, shooting her pistol into the air as she shouted, "I salute Kentucky Daisey's claim!"

Daisey participated in other land runs, including the 1892 opening of the Cheyenne-Arapaho Reservation, when she was sent away for trying to enter the territory too early, and the 1893 Cherokee Outlet opening. A newspaper reported that with the latter land run, Daisey had started a town called Bathsheba with more than thirty other women, though the story has been widely disputed over the years.

After the land runs came the oil.

Indigenous people were the first to discover the black liquid in Oklahoma. They used the natural oil and gas that seeped from the ground and settled on top of water sources as medicine for themselves and their animals. The Native Nations forced to relocate to the state heard about the oil that oozed from these sources (also known as "medicine springs") and began noting their location. Soon, people from nearby states would camp by the water to make use of the natural phenomenon.

Lewis Ross, brother of Cherokee chief John Ross, discovered oil in 1859 while drilling a deep saltwater well in the Cherokee Nation. The oil well he established provided as much as ten barrels a day for almost a year. Bartlesville, Oklahoma, the home of Phillips Petroleum Company, is named after Jacob H. Bartles, who operated a trading post; his employees George B. Keeler and William Johnstone would go on to make history as the first commercial oil well drillers. They did so with the help of the Cherokee Nation, which leased the land, and the Cudahy Oil Company, which did the actual drilling. This well, called Nellie Johnstone No. 1—named for William's daughter—produced fifty barrels of oil per day, but eventually the output surpassed the demand and storage availability, and the well was capped.

The Oklahoma oil boom truly began in 1899, when the railroad system arrived in Bartlesville. Over the following decade, the town ballooned from two hundred people to more than four thousand. Oil production increased as well, with the annual number of barrels growing from one thousand to more than forty-three million. Oklahoma produced the most oil in the mid-continent region from 1900 to 1935, and was second for another nine years; overall, the state produced nine hundred million barrels of oil during the entire period.

Perhaps the two most famous Bartlesville residents who earned their riches from oil are J. Paul Getty, who secured his first million from oil investment at the age of twenty-three and went on to build the J. Paul Getty Museum, which is part of the renowned Getty Center in Los Angeles; and Frank Phillips, founder of Phillips Petroleum Company, which was based in Bartlesville from 1917 until it merged with Conoco in the early 2000s.

Whites living in Indian Territory wanted to be citizens of the United States as early as the late nineteenth century. The real push for statehood began shortly after the land run of 1889, when thousands more settlers began moving into the area. The next year, the Organic Act of 1890 was established, which officially split present-day Oklahoma into Indian Territory and Oklahoma Territory. Per this law, a nonvoting delegate from Oklahoma Territory would be sent to the US House of Representatives.

Territory residents held several statehood conventions for nearly fifteen years, between 1891 and 1905, though they didn't all agree on how the state should be recognized. Some believed Oklahoma should have a single statehood, which would combine the two territories into one state. Others thought Oklahoma Territory and Indian Territory should operate as their own separate states. Some advocated for Oklahoma Territory to seek statehood without acknowledging Indian Territory whatsoever. And, finally, some residents were in favor of piecemeal absorption, which meant Oklahoma Territory would gain statehood immediately, and Native Nations throughout Indian Territory could be added individually.

Not all leaders within Indian Territory agreed on how statehood should be decided, either. While some believed Indian Territory should form its own state called Sequoyah, this hope was eventually squashed by the Curtis Act, which abolished tribal courts. This meant enforcing laws and court rulings of the Five Tribes of Oklahoma was defunct, and residents of Indian Territory were now held to federal law. Per this act, the United States president had to approve all tribal legislation passed after 1898.

President Theodore Roosevelt signed the Oklahoma Enabling Act into law in the summer of 1906. The act was in favor of single statehood, combining both territories into one state. The president was a Republican, and he and the Republican-controlled Congress believed it would be detrimental to the country if Indian Territory joined the Union as a Democratic state like its neighbors, Arkansas and Texas. The territories were tasked with drafting a state constitution, and also needed to set up one government. In September of the following year, both territories voted to establish a single statehood, and two months later, President Roosevelt made it official: Oklahoma joined the Union as the forty-sixth state on November 16, 1907.

When US Political Parties Switched Sides

Sometimes contemporary politicians will make reference to the Democratic Party having been the "proslavery party," and Republicans as "the party of Lincoln." While these descriptions are partially true, they lack vital context.

Back in the late 1800s, Republicans primarily controlled

states in the North and were the party responsible for helping implement state universities, a national currency, and the transcontinental railroad, among other initiatives. The Democrats controlled the South at that time, where they opposed post–Civil War Republican laws that protected and expanded the rights of newly freed Black Americans.

This all began to change in the 1930s, with the presidency of Democrat Franklin D. Roosevelt, who passed the New Deal to offset the detrimental effects of the Great Depression. The New Deal was a set of federal relief programs, such as welfare and infrastructure development, that favored bigger government, which had been, historically, a component of the Republican agenda. But FDR's progressive ideas were preceded by a Democratic presidential candidate named William Jennings Bryan, who, though he lost the election in 1896, ushered in traditionally Republican ideals of government involvement to attain social justice—a bid to win over states in the rapidly expanding West.

And thus began the realignment of political party views, wherein Republicans came to favor small government (meaning little to no government interaction in American lives) and Democrats supported social service programs funded by the federal government. President Lyndon B. Johnson, a Democrat, signed off on both the Civil Rights Act of 1964 and the Voting Rights Act of 1965. Over the next decade, white Southerners began to support the Republican Party in greater numbers, particularly in the wake of Richard Nixon's 1968 presidential campaign, wherein Republicans implemented the "Southern strategy," using overtly racist and faith-based appeals to win over white voters in the South who were appalled by the dismantling of Jim Crow laws.

Even before Oklahoma gained statehood in 1907, it had begun to put Jim Crow laws into place.

Originating in the South after the Civil War, Jim Crow laws, and the "Black codes" that preceded them, were a collection of various state and local legislation that enforced segregation in nearly all aspects of American life. They were used to subjugate Black Americans, who had recently gained their freedom from slavery, and forced them to live as second-class citizens. The name "Jim Crow" comes from a character in minstrel shows, a white man dressed in blackface who imitated and insulted Black Americans and their culture. Though the man who was responsible for the infamous character died a few years before slavery was abolished, Jim Crow laws would haunt Black people for the next century.

Oklahoma began by dividing white children and Black children into separate schools as early as 1897. Trains and streetcars were next; in 1908, these transportation companies were required to offer separate cars for both races. Fines for violating the law were steep, running as high as $1,000 for businesses that did not comply, $25 for passengers who did not sit in their assigned cars, and $500 for conductors who did not enforce segregation. That same year, the state declared it against the law for Black Americans to marry anyone "not of African descent." If a

Black person and a white person fell in love and ignored the law, they could be forced to pay $500 and sent to prison for up to five years. (This law was later expanded in 1921 to ban marriage between Black Americans and Indigenous people.)

The segregation laws grew over the next fifty years to include separate telephone booths (Oklahoma was the first state to implement this law), separate spaces in public libraries, separate boxing matches, separate health care and social service institutions, separate restrooms for people who worked in the mines, and even separate marching bands in parades, among others.

Through this legislation, Oklahoma developed a culture that was intolerant of the mere existence of Black Americans. And white Oklahomans readily enforced these laws, even though Black people had been living there since it was known as Indian Territory. Black Americans first made their way to Oklahoma with the forced migration of the Five Tribes. Several of the tribes, though they themselves were oppressed by white colonizers, also enslaved Black people and brought them to Oklahoma along the Trail of Tears.

The Cherokee Nation held the most enslaved people among the Five Tribes; by 1860, they reportedly owned 4,600 Black people. While this form of chattel slavery was similar to that practiced by white people, meaning the enslaved were forced to work long, difficult days tending to farmland, or in house jobs as servants and maids, the Cherokee used them in other ways, too. Black people were often made to serve as translators or interpreters if their slaveholders could not speak English, so that tribes could communicate and do business with white people.

Although some historians claim that the Indigenous people who enslaved Black people treated them more as indentured servants—a fixed term of slavery in which the enslaved often retained some rights—enslavement is enslavement. They were not free, nor were they treated as if they were free, as evidenced by the Slave Revolt of 1842, the largest rebellion of enslaved people in Indian Territory history.

On November 15 of that year, more than two dozen enslaved people in Webbers Falls, Oklahoma, decided enough was enough. At the Joseph Vann plantation, the enslaved waited until sleep had settled over the farm, then locked the slaveholders and overseers—supervisors who ensured the enslaved people "stayed in their place"—in their homes. The enslaved Black men, women, and children took all kinds of things that would help execute their rebellion: horses and mules, guns and ammunition, food, and other supplies. At sunrise, they headed out on their journey, stopping to pick up more enslaved people in Muscogee (Creek) Nation. The destination? Mexico, where they would be free.

Their trek was not without incident; at one point, the escapees fought Cherokee and Muscogee (Creek) pursuers, a battle that ended with two enslaved people dead and twelve captured. The rest of the group traveled on, managing to defend themselves against a duo of slave hunters in the Choctaw Nation—ultimately killing them. But, unfortunately, the story does not end with their freedom: Although nearly forty people had joined the rebellion, they were eventually outnumbered by their pursuers. Two days after the escape, the Cherokee National Council, afraid that word of the rebellion would spread and influence other enslaved people to revolt, approved a Cherokee militia of eighty-seven men, whose mission was to capture the fugitives and bring them back home. The runaways eventually lost their way and were caught by the militia near the Red River on November 28, after nearly two weeks on the run.

The remaining rebels were shuttled back to Webbers Falls in early December. Five of them were given a trial, found guilty of the two murders in Choctaw Nation, and executed. The rest of the group was sent back to their slaveholders. The Cherokee people believed the rebellion was sparked by free Black Seminole people, who were armed and lived nearby, at Fort Gibson, and so shortly after the runaways were caught, the Cherokee Nation passed "An Act in regard to Free Negroes," which forced all free Black Americans, with the exception of those who'd been formerly enslaved by the Cherokee people, to leave Cherokee land by January 1, 1843.

After the American Civil War ended in 1865, all enslaved people in Indian Territory were finally given their freedom; additionally, the Native Nations were ordered to provide land to the newly freed Black people. And from there, Black Oklahomans began to start businesses, and also purchased farmland.

For a time, they lived in relative harmony with their white neighbors in the post–Civil War Indian Territory. The state's land runs took place during this period of peace between Black and white Oklahomans, and perhaps explains why Black Americans were allowed to participate. Though the numbers have been debated for years, the 1890 Territorial Census of Oklahoma estimated around three thousand Black people lived in the state at the time, though only forty-two had joined the land run that year. However, some historians believe that the numbers of both white and Black homesteaders were inflated; the government wanted to promote the success of the newly settled land but also didn't want white people to think too many Black people were living there.

Meanwhile, Black Americans continued to flood into Oklahoma, primarily claiming land in Canadian, Blaine, and Kingfisher Counties. According to Lizzie Robinson, who traveled to the state in 1889 with a "train load of colored folk," most Black Boomers "built dugouts and small log houses to live in. They lived hard."

Around fifteen hundred Black Americans participated in the 1891 land run, which opened territory that had belonged to the Sac and Fox Nation. They came from Langston, an all-Black town named for John Mercer Langston, an African American congressman from Virginia. Their run was organized by Edward P. McCabe, an attorney and politician from Kansas who had founded Langston and whose goal was to make Oklahoma a majority-Black state that would not be controlled by white people. About a thousand Black people from that group ended up acquiring land. McCabe also ran a newspaper called the *Langston City Herald* and hired people to circulate it through Southern states, hoping to attract more Black Americans to the territory.

All-Black towns, also known as freedmen's towns, were far

from a rarity in the United States at that time, but they were especially abundant in Oklahoma. Black Americans, finally free from enslavement and looking for opportunities to start their lives anew, began moving into Indian Territory in 1865; by 1920, they had created more than fifty towns or settlements. These towns were also populated by the people formerly enslaved by members of the Five Tribes. Though some were short-lived, the following thirteen still exist today: Boley, Brooksville, Clearview, Grayson, Langston, Lima, Red Bird, Rentiesville, Summit, Taft, Tatums, Tullahassee, and Vernon.

Creating and building up these towns offered more opportunities for Black Americans, but it also provided comfort. In all-Black towns, they were safe from the violence and prejudice they were used to enduring from white people, and they could support one another by patronizing businesses owned and operated by other Black people. These efforts intensified as Oklahoma gained statehood and Jim Crow laws were passed. Black Oklahomans participated in education activism early on, organizing groups such as the Oklahoma State Federation of Negro Women's Clubs in 1910, which collaborated with other organizations to establish schools in Boley and Taft. Black women advocated for Black public libraries in Tulsa and Oklahoma City, and the Prince Hall Masons, a Black fraternal organization, worked with their women's group, the Order of the Eastern Star, to support college scholarships.

These all-Black towns were not only a great success for the time in which they existed, but they also set the stage for the Black Oklahomans who would one day establish Tulsa's remarkable Greenwood District. However, their towns eventually began to die out for a number of reasons, including white people who banned them from leasing land or working in their counties and also barred them from obtaining loans.

From the Indian Removal Act to land runs, and the oil boom to eventual statehood, Oklahoma saw its fair share of activity in the century after it was acquired through the Louisiana Purchase. Despite the state's commitment to segregation and inequality, Black Oklahomans found ways to not only survive but also thrive. This was a theme that would follow Black Americans through the forthcoming decades and one that had defined them since chattel slavery was abolished.

Mother remembers running down the street, six months pregnant with me, dodging bullets that were dropping all around her. She said that it was a miracle that she escaped alive and that I was later allowed to come into this world.

—**Julius Warren Scott**,
Tulsa Race Massacre survivor

2

To Be Black in America

On January 1, 1863, four million enslaved Black Americans in captured Confederate states were set free through President Abraham Lincoln's Emancipation Proclamation. Back in 1854, during Lincoln's Peoria Speech, he'd declared, "If the Negro is a man, why then my ancient faith teaches me that 'all men are created equal'; and that there can be no moral right in connection with one man's making a slave of another."

But as much as he may have personally hated slavery, Lincoln was initially quick to correct people who said the American Civil War was about abolishing the longstanding institution. His August 1862 editorial in the Washington, DC, newspaper the *Daily National Intelligencer* plainly stated: "My paramount object in this struggle *is* to save the Union, and is *not* either to save or to destroy slavery. If I could save the Union without freeing *any* slave I would do it, and if I could save it by freeing *all* the slaves I would do it; and if I could save it by freeing some and leaving others alone, I would also do that. What I do about slavery and the colored race, I do because I believe it helps to save the Union."

The Emancipation Proclamation sounds like an all-mighty document that immediately changed the lives of enslaved Black people in Southern rebel states, which had seceded from the Union beginning in 1860. But the executive order, issued in September 1862, was more of a symbolic gesture; the law said nothing about enslaved people in states and territories that were not part of the Confederacy, and no people were actually freed after the decree because the law was not constitutional. However, it did further clarify the aim of the Northern states in the war: It was no longer solely about preserving the Union. Now they were fighting a war of freedom.

Hearing the call for liberation, Black people—who had previously wanted to serve in the Union army but were banned by the government—began signing up to fight and entered combat after the Emancipation Proclamation went into effect in January 1863. About 200,000 Black Americans enlisted in the army and navy, despite the unequal pay, rules that prevented them from serving as officers, and the fact that they were forced to use secondhand uniforms and equipment.

While the Union and Confederate armies were battling each other in the last year of the Civil War, Lincoln was busy getting the Thirteenth Amendment to the Constitution passed in Congress—the law that would officially abolish slavery throughout the United States. The Senate passed the bill in April 1864, but the House of Representatives did not pass the amendment until nine months later, in January 1865, while the war raged on. Lincoln was assassinated on April 14, 1865, and died the next morning, just days after Confederate general Robert E. Lee surrendered to the Union army, but his legacy lived on through the symbol of the Emancipation Proclamation and the freedom afforded by the Thirteenth Amendment.

Lincoln also had a plan for Reconstruction, a period meant to reunify the country after the war. The Proclamation of Amnesty and Reconstruction, also known as the Ten Percent Plan, was issued in December 1863 and allowed any Confederate state with 10 percent of voters who swore allegiance to the Union to build new state governments and revise their state constitutions. It also protected the physical property (excluding enslaved Black people) of former plantation owners and pardoned all Southerners, except for top-level Confederate officials and military leaders, for secession from the Union.

But the Ten Percent Plan didn't lay out any citizenship rights or civil rights for Black people. In fact, it is believed that Lincoln's plan was created to be particularly attractive to Confederate states because he simply wanted to end the war and thought terms that didn't address Black citizenship would help persuade them to surrender. The strategy for what he apparently hoped would be a quick Reconstruction was never enacted, as the Ten Percent Plan was scrapped after Lincoln's assassination.

Radical Republicans in Congress believed Lincoln's Reconstruction plan was much too lenient on the rebel states; the plan they formulated was focused on providing equality to freed Black Americans. However, they did not find an ally in Andrew Johnson, who became president in April 1865 upon Lincoln's assassination and was a proud former slaveholder himself. Sometimes called an "accidental president," Johnson is widely considered in recent years to be one of the worst leaders in the history of the United States. He certainly didn't win over famous Black abolitionist Frederick Douglass, leaving a bad taste in Douglass's mouth when Johnson was sworn in as vice president in March 1865, a month before President Lincoln was killed. "Mr. Lincoln touched Mr. Johnson and pointed me out to him," Douglass wrote about the ceremony. "The first expression which came to his face, and which I think was the true index of his heart, was one of bitter contempt and aversion." Douglass turned to a friend and said, "Whatever Andrew Johnson may be, he is no friend of our race."

Johnson's political legacy supports Douglass's assessment. He consistently fought both Radical Republicans and more moderate politicians on every progressive policy, such as the Freedmen's Bureau, established to provide social services including health care, education, food, housing, and legal aid to freed Black Americans. The bureau was also committed to helping formerly enslaved people find new homes on land that had been abandoned or seized during the Civil War.

And though the House of Representatives overrode him, Johnson also vetoed the Civil Rights Act of 1866, which was Congress's first legislation on civil rights and granted citizenship to "all persons born in the United States"—excluding citizens of the Native Nations. The act was in part a response to the "Black codes," racist laws in Southern states that limited the freedom and job opportunities of Black Americans in the post–Civil War nation, while also punishing them for falsified crimes such as "vagrancy" if they were unemployed. (Sound familiar? They're a close relative of Jim Crow laws.) Johnson, who believed in states' rights, did nothing to curtail the discriminatory laws, forcing Congress to take action. In fact, his commitment to white supremacy was plainly stated in an 1866 letter to the governor of Missouri, in which Johnson wrote: "This is a country for white men, and by God, as long as I am president, it shall be a government for white men." It should be no surprise, then, that Johnson also opposed the Fourteenth Amendment, which provided the formerly enslaved with "equal protection" under the Constitution.

Despite President Johnson's persistent opposition to equality and voting rights for freed Black Americans, Congress moved forward with its plans for Radical Reconstruction, drafting the Reconstruction Acts of 1867–68. These acts included:

- Sending federal troops to all the rebel Southern states—with the exception of Tennessee, the first to be readmitted to the Union in July 1866—so they could be ruled under military law.

- The revision of rebel state constitutions with both Black and white delegates present at the convention where the rewriting would take place.

- A commitment to Black suffrage (i.e., giving Black men the right to vote), and the requirement for rebel states to ratify the Fourteenth Amendment before they were readmitted to the Union.

The Fifteenth Amendment, passed in 1870, granted Black men the Constitutional right to vote, guaranteeing they would not be prevented from casting a ballot "on account of race, color, or previous condition of servitude."

The Reconstruction laws and amendments passed by the Radical Republicans were groundbreaking, but the Fifteenth Amendment was an absolute game changer in terms of democracy. Not only could Black men now vote, but since there was nothing preventing them from running for political office, they could help elect Black people, as well.

And that's exactly what they did.

The former Confederate states saw record numbers of Black men running for political office—and winning. Elected in 1870, Hiram Rhodes Revels of Mississippi was the first Black US senator; that same year, Joseph Rainey, who was born into slavery in South Carolina, was elected by the state as the first Black man in the House of Representatives. By 1877, around two thousand African Americans held positions in local, state, and federal office in the rebel states, just twelve years after the end of the Civil War. These unprecedented numbers of Black leaders are largely credited for the dismantling of the Black codes.

The first Black US Senator and US Representatives, in the 41st and 42nd Congress, L to R: Hiram R. Revels, Benjamin S. Turner, Robert C. De Large, Josiah T. Walls, Jefferson F. Long, Joseph H. Rainey, and Robert B. Elliott

This enraged proslavery white Southerners, who were furious that the source of their labor and wealth had been set free and were now enfranchised. They believed the racist notions that had allowed slavery to thrive for centuries: that Africans and African Americans were unintelligent, wild, incapable of leadership, and fit only for hard manual labor and domestic work. Or, if they didn't truly believe this in their hearts, they behaved as if they did, perpetuating the system of white supremacy the United States had been built upon.

Now that slavery was illegal and they saw Black Americans

making political, social, and economic gains, they felt victimized. Since the founding of the United States, racists have felt threatened by laws meant to expand justice and equality—they see the legislation as a roadblock to their own success, rather than something that provides people with the human rights they've always deserved. Further, they were nervous about the political alignment of poor white people and freed Black people.

Poor whites resented the "planter elite," or wealthy plantation owners; too poor to have purchased enslaved people prior to the Civil War themselves, they didn't benefit from slavery. This likely stung even more due to the lie of white supremacy that told them they were entitled to whatever they wanted simply because of their skin color. Some were so disillusioned that they began to associate with freed Black people; in reality, poor Southern white people often had more in common with Black Americans at the time than either of them did with the well-off white men who'd held the vast majority of political and economic power in the country since its inception. They also benefited from some Reconstruction policies, such as the Homestead Act of 1862, which gave any American citizen—Black and white alike—a "fair chance" by allowing them to buy land.

Unfortunately, the goals and policies of Reconstruction soon began to lose steam. With heavy concentration in the South due to chattel slavery, freed Black people made up the majority of Republican voters in the former Confederate states; however, Black politicians were never able to achieve any sort of majority in state governments during Reconstruction, limiting their power and influence. Further, Democrats began to pass laws that made it difficult if not impossible for Black people and poor white people to vote or be elected, including poll taxes, literacy tests, and residency requirements. Once the right to vote was taken away, those same disenfranchised Americans were also prevented from running for local office or serving on a jury.

President Andrew Johnson is surely a mascot for the failure of Reconstruction; his racism and refusal to hold states accountable only served to undermine the tireless efforts of Congress. He was also the first president to be impeached—convicted of charges for a crime or misconduct while in office—after violating the Tenure of Office Act, which didn't allow him to fire federal officials who'd been approved by the Senate without Senate approval. He narrowly missed being removed from office by the Senate in 1868—by *one* vote.

There were other factors to blame for the mishandling of Reconstruction efforts, as well, including an economic depression in 1873, which led to widespread unemployment and bankruptcy; waning commitment to racial equality from white people, including Northerners, some of whom had fought alongside Black Americans in the Union army; and President Rutherford B. Hayes's 1877 removal of the military from former Confederate states, which allowed white Southerners to start a decades-long campaign to disenfranchise and terrorize Black people through violence and other means.

In Oklahoma, A. C. Hamlin became the first Black politician elected to the state legislature in 1908, just a year after the territory gained statehood. He represented a district in Logan County, which was primarily Black at the time. The son of formerly enslaved people, Hamlin saw success during his time in government: a law he wrote helped create the Industrial Institute for the Deaf, Blind, and Orphans of the Colored Race in the all-Black town of Taft, and he sponsored a bill that would enforce equal conditions for Black railroad passengers.

But instead of seeing this as much-needed progress in the decades after Reconstruction, white politicians and constituents remained threatened by Black Americans gaining even an ounce of political power. The white politicians serving alongside Hamlin wasted no time in trying to ensure he would not be reelected—and that no Black legislator would follow in his footsteps—by passing laws that made it more difficult for Black Americans to vote. One of these efforts was the state's Voter Registration Act of 1910, which included a grandfather clause that required a literacy test for all voters—except for those who were able to vote on January 1, 1866, as well as their ancestors and descendants. You know who weren't able to legally vote until 1870? Black people. Therefore, the law excluded many Black Oklahomans from voting, as Black Americans had historically been lawfully prevented from learning to read and write or forced to attend inadequate, woefully underfunded schools. This crooked legislation also allowed voting registrars to turn away Black voters at their discretion, without ever giving them the test.

Sure enough, A. C. Hamlin lost when he ran for reelection in 1910.

Oklahoma's Voter Registration Act was overturned by the US Supreme Court five years later in *Guinn v. United States*, but it was too late for Hamlin to try again for a second term. He died in 1912 at the age of thirty-one.

As the gains Black people made during Reconstruction faded away or were overturned completely, tensions increased even more between Black and white Americans. Black codes and Jim Crow laws had become the rule of the South, and Northern states were home to plenty of racism and segregation, as well. White people had now seen what Black Americans could achieve when they were treated as equal citizens—and many of them didn't like it. They feared free, educated Black people; perhaps they were convinced that if Black Americans gained equality and political power, they would treat white people the same way they themselves had treated African Americans for centuries. Whatever the reason, violence and terrorism inflicted on Black Americans increased greatly in the years after Reconstruction—and no single organization was more responsible for or emblematic of this white supremacist resurgence than the Ku Klux Klan.

The KKK was founded by Confederate veterans in Pulaski, Tennessee, immediately after the Civil War ended as a social club for those bitter about the new freedoms afforded to formerly enslaved Black people. Before long, there were branches of the Klan in nearly every former rebel state, and their influence was so widespread and their terrorism so violent that Congress eventually passed three acts to suppress the group. The KKK disbanded in the 1870s as Reconstruction ended; with Southern states left to their own devices and the subsequent surge of Jim Crow laws, the Klan's work was being done. Black people were disenfranchised, unable to fully enjoy their freedom, and lived in perpetual terror of violence, especially lynching.

However, the KKK reemerged decades later, due in large part to a film created during the rise of Hollywood cinema: D. W. Griffith's *The Birth of a Nation* was one of history's first blockbusters, and memorable scenes painted KKK members as heroes—heroes who were "saving" white women from Black men—instead of the violent villains they were, inspiring legions of white men around the country. So powerful was its influence that *The Birth of a Nation* was the first movie to ever be screened at the White House, during President Woodrow Wilson's first term. Wilson, who segregated federal government offices to appease Southern conservatives, supposedly said about the film: "It's like writing history with lightning. And my only regret is that it is all terribly true."

Atlanta preacher and colonel William J. Simmons felt the same way and, fueled by Griffith's film, as well as Thomas Dixon's book *The Clansman*, was determined to restore the Klan to what he saw as their glory days. In 1915, Simmons and over a dozen other men gathered at Georgia's Stone Mountain on Thanksgiving night and burned a wooden cross—one of the Klan's trademark fear tactics. It was official: the Ku Klux Klan was back.

And this time, the target of their hatred wasn't only Black people but also Jewish people, Catholics, and anyone they considered "foreign." The new version of the KKK was intent on narrowing the vision of who they considered "real Americans"; they were intimidated by immigrants moving to the United States and also fearful of a communist revolution, like that of the Bolsheviks in Russia. This created the myth of them as heroes in the eyes of many white people, who believed the KKK to be patriots who were simply trying to save the country from people they'd come to see as enemies, to return the nation to the "good old days" of the Old South.

. Although Klan members have often been portrayed as poor, uneducated white Americans, the new KKK counted people of many occupations and socioeconomic levels among its ranks, including attorneys, doctors, and clergy. All around the country, even in Northern states like Ohio and Pennsylvania, the Klan's membership was growing by the hundred thousands. The terrorist group became so powerful that members eventually held political office in various states, including Indiana and Colorado.

The KKK began to set up shop in Oklahoma in the early 1900s. By December 1921, the Tulsa branch reportedly had 3,200 members. It also prided itself on a separate group for women, as well as a KKK branch for children, available to boys ages twelve to eighteen. And in the early 1920s, soon after the Tulsa Race Massacre, several Tulsa city and county representatives were known Klansmen.

The existence of the KKK and the unchecked violence against Black people they encouraged begs the question: Where were the police?

The history of policing in the United States is complex, with roots dating back to slavery, but the very first public police forces were founded in the seventeenth century. Operating in Boston and New Amsterdam (present-day New York City), the forces were initially organized as part-time night watchmen. However, throughout the rest of the colonies, police forces were privately funded, a system adopted from the English. The night-watchmen arrangement was somewhat problematic, in that some of them were doing the job as punishment for their own crimes and some drank alcohol or even napped while they were supposed to be on watch. Their main duties involved cracking down on gambling and sex workers.

Boston was the first to create an official, publicly funded police department, in 1838, founded out of a need to protect businesses and goods shipped from the city's port. Looking to the London Metropolitan Police as an example of how to operate, several cities also used this model when they established their own departments shortly thereafter, including New Orleans, Cincinnati, Philadelphia, Chicago, Milwaukee, Baltimore, and Newark. Their primary goals were to stop criminal activity and disorderly behavior.

Southern states, however, were a different story. While Northern cities such as Boston were primarily in the business of shipping, the South was in the business of agriculture, driven by slave labor. And slaveholders wanted to be sure the people they were enslaving wouldn't jeopardize their business by running away or revolting, so they created slave patrols: the first of what we would consider to be police forces in the South. South

Carolina was the first state to implement a slave patrol, in 1704, and other states soon followed.

Slave patrols took many forms; depending on the area, they were made up of white volunteers, guards, police departments, or even state militia who were solely focused on the persecution of enslaved people (and freed Black people, in some cases). They searched for runaways and doled out brutal punishments to those who were found, as well as those who were reported to be causing trouble on the plantation. Patrollers had few, if any, restrictions when it came to upholding the institution of slavery; they were even allowed to force their way into homes where they believed enslaved people were hiding, without any reason or warrant.

Although there was no need for official slave patrols once the Confederacy lost the war and slavery was abolished, their focus on targeting Black Americans lived on. Instead of capturing enslaved people who'd run away and ensuring plantation rules were followed, Southern police during Reconstruction tasked themselves with enforcing Black codes and segregation, ultimately doing whatever they could to limit the rights and progress of freed Black people.

As their job had never been to protect or serve Black Americans—essentially the opposite—police officers often looked the other way when it came to the actions of white terrorists like the KKK or other vigilantes who intimidated and violated the Black community. White mobs routinely carried out violence against Black people without intervention; lynchings went unpunished, even when members of the police departments had heard about plans for them in advance. In fact, the KKK and the police have a long, intertwined history. While the group claimed its vigilante justice was saving Americans from crime the police force wasn't tackling, the Klan was often working in tandem with the police to carry out its violence. Throughout the country, the KKK has counted police officers among its membership, collaborating on lynchings, intimidation like cross burning, and other forms of terrorism.

During his campaign in 1922, Walter M. Pierce, who would be sworn in as Oregon governor the following year, was openly endorsed by the KKK, as were the Portland sheriff, chief of police, district and US attorneys, and the mayor. Together, they worked with the terrorist group to limit the rights of Catholics and Japanese immigrants in particular. These actions were in line with Oregon's racist history—dating back to 1844, before it was even part of the United States—when it passed a "lash law" forcing all Black people, enslaved or freed, to leave the state or "receive upon his or her bare back not less than twenty nor more than thirty-nine stripes." (Just five years later, in 1849, Black people were banned from moving into or even visiting the state.)

The Klan also has law enforcement roots in Anaheim, California, where in the early 1920s, residents elected four Klansmen to the five-member city council, which allowed its members who were also police officers to parade around in full KKK regalia during their shifts. So while it may seem shocking that the KKK was allowed to terrorize and murder with abandon, in fact their actions were sometimes approved of or even carried out by police officers themselves, and the governments that oversaw and funded them.

A key symbol associated with the KKK is the noose, and for good reason. *Lynching,* a term for any murder committed to punish an alleged crime without administering a fair trial, was a common form of vigilante justice in the late 1800s and early 1900s; it manifested primarily as death by hanging (often preceded by torture and burning). Both white and Black people were at risk of being lynched for a number of perceived offenses, but in the South, lynching was systematically used as intimidation by white people who were angry that Black Americans had gained their freedom en masse. They wanted to keep Black people "in their place," and the fear of being killed by a mob for trivial, unproven, or fabricated offenses often did just that.

Before Oklahoma gained statehood, lynching was often used to punish criminals, as the territories lacked formal court systems and police departments. From 1885 to 1907, most victims were white, and they were usually lynched for such crimes—or suspected crimes—as robbing stagecoaches and trains, gambling, and theft of livestock. However, after Oklahoma became a state in 1907, established branches of state government, and began enforcing Jim Crow laws, nearly all lynching victims were Black.

The allegations against Black men in particular were often sexual assault, rape, or murder. However, many if not most of these claims were false and used as an excuse to justify the lynchings by vengeful white supremacists. The accusations were often born out of a completely innocent interaction, such as a fleeting look or accidental touch; this is what many believe happened between Dick Rowland and Sarah Page in that Tulsa elevator in 1921. But, sometimes, a Black man who'd been in a consensual but secret relationship with a white woman was accused of rape when the truth came out to preserve the white woman's reputation or to save her from punishment by white supremacists. Historian Philip Dray wrote: "Whites could not countenance the idea of a white woman *desiring* sex with a Negro, thus any physical relationship between a white woman and a black man had, by definition, to be an unwanted assault."

The "safety of white women" was not only a major focus—and thinly veiled justification—of vigilante violence, but in states such as Louisiana, white women were the *only* women protected against rape by law. Black women, who had been habitually raped and sexually abused during slavery, were not protected by the law, whether enslaved or free. Louisiana also enforced a law calling for the execution of any enslaved Black man *accused* of raping or attempting to rape a white woman. Southern writer and eventual politician Rebecca Latimer Felton said in 1897, "If it takes lynching to protect women's dearest possession from drunken, ravening human beasts, then I say lynch a thousand a week." To be sure, Felton, an outspoken white supremacist, was referring only to the protection of white women like herself.

In June 1920, six young Black men in Duluth, Minnesota, working with the John Robinson Circus, were accused of raping a young white woman while holding her white boyfriend at gunpoint. A family physician who examined the woman the next morning found no evidence of sexual assault or rape, but that didn't stop authorities from arresting the Black men and throwing them in jail. Although the accusations, reported by local newspapers, were enough to put these men in serious danger, the situation was further enflamed by a fast-spreading, completely false rumor that the woman had died from the alleged assault.

Black people were a tiny percentage of the Duluth population at the time—just 495 of the city's 98,000 residents were African American. The city discriminated against its small Black population in many ways, including lower pay and unequal housing conditions. Between the allegations, the rumors, and the fact that many white people in Duluth resented Black people for moving from the South to work at the local branch of the United States Steel Corporation, a white mob thousands strong quickly formed outside the police station, where the men were being held. The white people broke into the jail, using heavy logs and bricks to smash windows and bust down doors. There, they reportedly held a mock trial for the six Black men; found three of them—Isaac McGhie, Elmer Jackson, and Elias Clayton—guilty of rape; beat them; and hanged them from a light pole a block away. The remaining three men in jail were protected by the Minnesota National Guard, then shuttled to the county jail in St. Louis the next day, along with other Black "suspects" working in the circus, to prevent more lynchings. No one from the white mob was ever charged or convicted of the three murders.

Ida B. Wells-Barnett

One of history's most well-known anti-lynching activists was a Black woman named Ida Bell Wells-Barnett. Born into slavery in Holly Springs, Mississippi, on July 16, 1862, Wells was orphaned at age sixteen due to the yellow fever epidemic

(which also claimed her infant brother), and became the primary caregiver for her younger siblings through her work as an educator. She moved her family to Memphis, Tennessee, where she continued teaching. Wells fought racism early on, filing a lawsuit against a train company for discrimination in 1884; she won a $500 settlement, though the decision was later overturned. Publishing under the pseudonym "Iola," Wells began writing about Southern race and political matters, and became publisher of the *Memphis Free Speech and Headlight* and *Free Speech*. In 1891, she was fired from her teaching position because of her frequent criticism about the unequal conditions of Memphis's segregated schools.

The next year, after her friend Thomas Moss was lynched for trying to defend his business, Wells began speaking out against the practice in her editorials and traveled throughout the South collecting information on recent lynchings. In May 1892, while she was visiting New York, a mob of white men destroyed her newspaper office, threatening to lynch her if she ever returned to Memphis. She briefly remained in New York, writing a comprehensive report on lynching for the Black newspaper the *New York Age*, before moving to Chicago. Over the years, Wells achieved one milestone after another, such as founding the National Association of Colored Women in 1896, serving as the first secretary of the National Afro-American Council, and cofounding the National Association for the Advancement of Colored People—though she eventually left after deeming the group too politically moderate. Wells founded the Alpha Suffrage Club in 1913 in Chicago and defied racist white suffragettes from the South when she marched beside them—rather than behind them—at that year's Woman Suffrage Parade.

She married attorney Ferdinand Barnett—hyphenating her name in a time when few women would consider it—and had four children. Wells-Barnett died on March 25, 1931, in Chicago, from kidney disease. She appeared on a US Postal Service stamp in 1990, and in 2019, Chicago renamed a major thoroughfare Ida B. Wells Drive, the first major street in the city to commemorate a Black woman. In 2020, Wells-Barnett posthumously received a Pulitzer Prize for "outstanding and courageous reporting." She likely would have been pleased with this honor, as she is quoted as saying, "I'd rather go down in history as one lone Negro who dared to tell the government that it had done a dastardly thing than to save my skin by taking back what I said."

According to the Oklahoma Historical Society, which obtained data from the Tuskegee Institute and the National Association for the Advancement of Colored People, 147 people were lynched in Oklahoma from 1885 to 1930. Fifty of them were reported to be Black; however, the actual number of Black people killed is likely much higher due to the fact that many lynchings went unreported. And while the number was decreasing, when Oklahoma entered the Roaring Twenties, vigilante justice and mob violence were still prevalent.

Three violent events that took place in Oklahoma in 1920 may have been clues as to what was in store for Tulsa just a year later.

In August, a young white taxi driver named Homer Nida was shot and robbed by three white passengers, a woman and two men, who told him they were headed to a dance in the Red Fork community of Tulsa. One of the men shot Nida in the stomach, pushed him out of the taxi, and left him to die on the side of the road. Nida was soon found by someone driving by the scene and taken to the hospital to be treated for his wounds.

The next day, after bragging publicly about knowing one of the people involved in the crime, a young man named Roy Belton, who had a gun on him, was arrested in nearby Nowata and taken to Tulsa in police custody. Still in the hospital, Nida identified Belton, who was also known as Tom Owens, as one of his attackers. At first, Belton denied it, but his alibi fell apart when the woman he'd supposedly spent the evening with admitted to being in the cab and offered up Belton as the shooter. Belton eventually confessed, though he claimed the shooting was an accident.

Knowing the jail could be mobbed if Nida died, Sheriff James Woolley installed extra guards. But it was no use. When Nida succumbed to his injuries and Belton pleaded not guilty, a mob a thousand people strong stormed the jail with guns. The sheriff apparently tried to deter them, saying, "Let the law take its course, boys. The electric chair will get him before long, but you know this is no way to interfere with the law." However, the mob would not be stopped. They kidnapped Belton at gunpoint, forcing the sheriff to release him from the top floor, where the jail usually housed Black prisoners to keep them safe from exactly what was happening to Belton.

"We got him, boys," members of the mob announced as they marched Belton outside.

The Tulsa police force followed the mob as they drove him outside city limits, but they didn't do anything to protect Belton; though they should have been the ones to stop the illegal violence that was certain to take place, they were under strict instructions not to get involved. Police chief John Gustafson believed "any demonstration from an officer would have started gun play and dozens of innocent people would have been killed and injured." One report claims the police were directing traffic during the event for a procession of cars that was "nearly a mile long."

Roy Belton was given a cigarette in his last few moments, then hanged beneath a sign for a tire company. As was often the custom of lynchings, spectators took pieces of clothing and rope as souvenirs. Chief Gustafson expressed regret about the murder, claiming he did "not condone mob law" and that he was "absolutely opposed to it," but in the same breath stated, "It is my honest opinion that the lynching of Belton will prove of real benefit to Tulsa and [the] vicinity. It was an object lesson to the hijackers and auto thieves, and I believe it will be taken as such."

Sheriff Woolley agreed, saying it showed criminals "that the men of Tulsa mean business."

The Black newspaper the *Tulsa Star* expressed concern about Belton's murder. If vigilantes were so quick to lynch a white man, that gave the Black community little reason to believe they wouldn't be next—even though no Black person had yet been lynched in Tulsa. The paper's editor, A. J. Smitherman, wrote: "There is no crime, however atrocious, that justifies mob violence." In contrast, the white newspapers the *Tulsa Tribune* and *Tulsa World* sided with the mob, sheriff, and police chief, with the latter going so far as to say the lynching "will not be the last by any means."

The paper's prediction came true. Just a day after Belton was murdered, a young Black man named Claude Chandler was lynched in Oklahoma City, a mere one hundred miles away. Three police officers had raided Chandler's home, where he and his family made moonshine. These were the early days of Prohibition, when the US government banned the sale and production of alcohol. A shootout had ensued, and Chandler's father died, as did one of the officers. Chandler was accused of murder and thrown into jail, but, same as Belton, he was removed by vigilantes seeking their own justice. Members of the Black community got word of the kidnapping and set out to save Chandler, but they were too late. The next day, around lunchtime, they found Chandler's body, beaten and shot, hanged from a tree a few miles outside Oklahoma City.

Not even six months later, on December 6, 1920, the *New York Times* reported that "an unidentified Negro . . . was taken from the Hughes County [Oklahoma] jail" the previous evening "by a mob of about fifty men and hanged to a telephone pole." His alleged crime? Raping a sixty-seven-year-old white woman. According to the report, deputy sheriffs found him about a mile from the woman's house, and the man "fired on the officers." His lynched body was later found "riddled with bullets," at least three of which came from the arresting officers. In the one hundred years since his murder, the lynching victim has been referred to only as "unnamed" or "unidentified."

Any Oklahomans paying attention—but especially Black Americans—were well aware that the Oklahoma lynchings of 1920 did not bode well for the future. They knew the worst was yet to come.

In fact, it had already begun.

If we must die, let it not be like hogs
Hunted and penned in an inglorious spot,
While round us bark the mad and hungry dogs,
Making their mock at our accursèd lot.
If we must die, O let us nobly die,
So that our precious blood may not be shed
In vain; then even the monsters we defy
Shall be constrained to honor us though dead!
O kinsmen! we must meet the common foe!
Though far outnumbered let us show us brave,
And for their thousand blows deal one death-blow!
What though before us lies the open grave?
Like men we'll face the murderous, cowardly pack,
Pressed to the wall, dying, but fighting back!

—"If We Must Die," Claude McKay, July 1919

3

Fighting for Survival

Two years before the Tulsa massacre, the United States was host to more than three dozen so-called race riots—a collection of events that would come to be known as the Red Summer, a term created by James Weldon Johnson, a leader of the National Association for the Advancement of Colored People (NAACP). While race riots sound as if they were acts of violence that broke out between different racial groups, they're more complicated than that. In actuality, race riots were often coordinated attacks against Black communities by white mobs who felt they needed to take justice into their own hands for perceived or fabricated offenses. When Black people fought back to defend themselves, the story was often twisted and called a riot, rather than the blatant attacks that they were.

The early 1900s were a time of major change for Black Americans. Fed up with their unequal treatment and lack of opportunities in the South, many packed up their belongings and moved their families to the North, Midwest, and West. Known as the Great Migration, an estimated six million Black Americans left Southern states between 1915 and 1970 to start new lives. Before this mass exodus, 90 percent of Black Americans lived in the Southern states in which they or their ancestors had been enslaved; now they headed to cities like Chicago, New York, Detroit, and Philadelphia, which were facing labor shortages in manufacturing and industrial jobs. Though families were sometimes able to make the trip together, other people were forced to travel alone to find employment and a place to stay; once someone had settled into their new home, their family and friends often joined them, resulting in vast increases of the Black population throughout the United States.

Although, historically, racism is often painted as a Southern problem, many Black people were treated just as poorly after they migrated to the North. They may have escaped the Jim Crow laws that kept everything from restaurants to water fountains to schools "separate but equal," but Northern cities were not free of bigotry. White people weren't always eager to see Black people in their neighborhoods or working beside them, and they didn't hide it. But Black people continued to move out of the South in droves, for opportunities that ranged from regular employment to voting without intimidation or violence.

The main reason for the labor shortage in the North was the Great War, or what we know today as World War I. Employers often hired immigrants to fill jobs at factories, steel mills, and railroads, but due to fewer Europeans moving to the United States during the war, these jobs remained open. And Black people were more than willing to scoop them up as they began their new lives in the North.

Additionally, millions of Americans traveled overseas to fight after the United States entered World War I in 1917. President Woodrow Wilson, who declared war on Germany that April, said, "The world must be made safe for democracy." Not just Europe, but the *world*—which included the United States, and should have, therefore, included its Black citizens, who'd been working tirelessly for equality at home. Not everyone believed in the cause; some found it hypocritical that a country that didn't treat Black Americans equally would ask them to fight on its behalf. Still, hundreds of thousands of Black Americans served their country in World War I, hopeful that things would change back home soon, too.

Despite being enslaved for centuries, then segregated and treated as second-class citizens, Black Americans have fought for the United States in every war in which it's participated. And during World War I, in particular, Black Americans felt they had something to prove. The Civil War had been about fighting for freedom, but now they were fighting for respect. Signing up to serve their country would show they were loyal to the United

States—that they were patriots, just like the white men joining the military beside them.

At the start of the war, Black men could serve in one of four all-Black regiments: the Ninth and Tenth Cavalry, and the Twenty-Fourth and Twenty-Fifth Infantry. Although Black people were allowed to serve in several positions throughout the army, most African American soldiers were assigned to service units, which were more labor-intensive. Earning a role in combat was nearly unheard of for Black Americans until the War Department finally created two primarily Black combat divisions in 1917: the Ninety-Second Division, which was made up of military officers as well as those who'd been drafted, and the Ninety-Third Division, which mostly comprised National Guard units hailing from Chicago, Cleveland, Massachusetts, New York, and Washington, DC. That same year, the army also established an all-Black training camp for officers in Des Moines, Iowa, which trained more than twelve hundred men in its first class but closed soon after, due to the War Department concluding the instruction was "poor and inadequate."

Despite the fact that they were allowed to hold prestigious positions in the army, Black Americans were still treated poorly. Black officers were disrespected by white men of lower rank who refused to salute them, and they were turned away from officers' clubs. Black soldiers often had to wear decades-old uniforms for months on end, were forced to sleep outside in tents rather than the barracks—buildings used to house servicemen—where white soldiers slept, and had to eat outside during the colder months because they were not allowed to sit in the mess halls. However, though they received the least amount of respect, they continued to work hard to prove they deserved to be serving their country.

The combat soldiers were treated somewhat better than the laborers, though they faced their own challenges. The Ninety-Second Division was forced to train at separate locations (rather than all together, as a cohesive group) before heading overseas because, according to the Army Historical Foundation, the War Department was worried about racial uprisings if they all trained together. The Ninety-Second Division also had to endure lies about their performance on the battlefield by racist white American officers. Composed of about fifteen thousand officers and soldiers, the Ninety-Second Division was known as the Buffalo Soldiers; fighting primarily in France, they were awarded several medals and honors from the French military. But they were not the first Black combat troops to fight in France—that honor was held by the Ninety-Third Division. Its 369th Infantry, also known as the Harlem Hellfighters, fought in major operations throughout France, received a military award from the French army, and formed a band that became popular throughout Europe, introducing the continent to American jazz music. The Black Devils, or the 370th Infantry, received multiple military awards as well, including Distinguished Service Crosses, a Distinguished Service Medal, and a French military award. It was also the only

Black regiment to include all Black officers. The 372nd Infantry received a French military award for its fearless combat skills and its actions during an operation that was integral to ending the war.

Back home, Black women were also instrumental to the First World War. Through the National Association of Colored Women—founded by Ida B. Wells-Barnett—they led rallies, raised more than $5 million in war bonds, and lent emotional support to African American soldiers.

According to author and critic Harper Barnes, the "first major race riot of the World War I period" occurred in East St. Louis, Illinois, in July 1917—and many attribute it directly to tensions caused by the Great Migration. White workers at the Aluminum Ore Company had gone on strike that spring, but instead of meeting the workers' terms, the company replaced the white laborers with Black employees who were new to town and willing to do the work. In May, resentful workers began filing "formal complaints"—most of them likely false or exaggerated in scope—about Black people, and after a report that a Black man with a gun had attempted to rob a white man in the city, mobs of white people began beating African Americans in the streets. They even took to their cars, organizing drive-by attacks to shoot into houses and stores in Black neighborhoods. These drive-bys were spurred by false news reports in local papers that Black Americans were committing crimes, some as serious as rape—and white people had taken it upon themselves to seek justice.

The National Guard was eventually called in to help stop the violence, but the troops were sent home in June, and the attacks resumed. On July 1, after a white man driving a Model T fired shots into houses where Black people lived, some African Americans shot at another Model T cruising through the neighborhood. What they didn't know was that the two men in the second car weren't there to terrorize them—they were, instead, undercover police officers in an unmarked car who were there to look into the drive-by that had occurred earlier.

The fact that the people who'd shot at them had made a mistake to protect their neighborhood didn't matter—the Black community in East St. Louis would pay the price. Over three days in early July, dozens of people were killed by a white mob. Official reports say that thirty-nine of them were Black, a total that included children—though some reports state that as many as one hundred Black people were killed. Hundreds more were injured as they were yanked off streetcars and beaten with clubs. Fire was used as a weapon, too; the structures the mob set ablaze amounted to nearly $375,000 worth of damages—the equivalent of several millions of dollars today—and destroyed the livelihood of the Black community.

The massacre, along with recent lynchings in Memphis, Tennessee, and Waco, Texas, prompted a relatively new group called the NAACP to organize the Negro Silent Protest Parade. Held on July 28, 1917, in New York City, the parade drew nearly ten thousand protesters from across the country. In attendance was activist, writer, and educator W. E. B. Du Bois, as well as NAACP leader James Weldon Johnson, author of the poem "Lift Ev'ry Voice and Sing," which was later set to music by his brother, John Rosamond Johnson, and became known as the Black National Anthem.

Organized by the NAACP, the Negro Silent Protest Parade, held on July 28, 1917, in New York City, protested the recent spate of lynchings and murders in Waco, Texas; Memphis, Tennessee; and East St. Louis, Illinois. Nearly ten thousand protesters marched silently down Fifth Avenue, including co-organizers James Weldon Johnson and W. E. B. Du Bois.

Pray for the Lady Macbeths of East St. Louis

Protest signs have long been a clever, concise, and effective way to call for desired social change. During the Negro Silent Protest Parade organized by the NAACP in 1917, marchers carried signs bearing messages such as:

YOUR HANDS ARE FULL OF BLOOD

MOTHERS, DO LYNCHERS GO TO HEAVEN?

MR. PRESIDENT, WHY NOT MAKE AMERICA SAFE FOR DEMOCRACY?

PRAY FOR THE LADY MACBETHS OF EAST ST. LOUIS

The last sign may not make as much sense today as it did to people back then. The National Humanities Center defines "Lady Macbeths" as the white women in East St. Louis who shouted encouragement to the mob that was beating and killing the Black community, much like the woman who encouraged her husband to carry out violence and murder in the Shakespeare play *Macbeth*. In some cases, they took their participation a step further, joining the men in attacking Black people during the massacre.

According to the newspaper the *Cleveland Advocate*, these white women "pursued the [Black] women who were driven out of the burning homes with the idea . . . of inflicting added pain, if possible. They stood around in groups, laughing and jeering, while they witnessed the final writhings of the terror and pain" of the victims. The protest sign, then, can be seen as a facetious take on the situation, or perhaps a sincere call to be magnanimous and show compassion for the women who, though often portrayed as passive or submissive, were just as guilty as their white male counterparts.

The NAACP, one of the nation's oldest civil rights organizations, was itself founded as a response to a race riot that took place nine years before the East St. Louis massacre, in a city nearly one hundred miles north: Springfield, Illinois. In August 1908, word began to circulate there that a Black man had sexually assaulted a white woman. A white mob quickly gathered in front of the city jail, where they demanded the police turn over a Black suspect who had been arrested for the alleged crime, as well as another imprisoned Black man who was being held on a charge of murdering a white railroad engineer. Prepared for the possibility of a mob, the Springfield police had managed to sneak the Black men from the jail and drive them out of town to avoid what would surely have been a double lynching.

The white mob was furious that they wouldn't get their chance with the prisoners—and in response, they incited a riot. Over the next few days, they destroyed property of the white man who'd provided the car to transfer the Black men out of town; looted and destroyed a Black business district in downtown Springfield; and lynched two Black men, one who was elderly. Troops were sent in to help curb the violence, but white people continued to attack Black Springfieldians over the next few weeks. When it was all over, the white mob had killed six people—four white, two Black—and injured dozens of others; caused property damage that amounted to hundreds of thousands of dollars; and displaced more than forty Black families whose homes they had burned.

The white rioters, well aware that they had caused such

violence in the town where President Abraham Lincoln once lived, reportedly shouted, "Lincoln freed you, now we'll show you where you belong!" Historians have identified a pattern in that the rioters would attack and loot the homes of successful Black people—business owners, real estate workers, and government employees. The two Black men they killed had been financially successful homeowners. An unnamed Black woman, who had been a child at the time of the riot, later said, "See, the people that they harmed and hurt were not really the no-gooders. They were very busy hurting the prominent. . . . There was a great deal of animosity toward any well-established Negro who owned his house and had a good job."

Fed up with lynchings and other anti-Black violence and behavior, a group of white people organized a meeting to discuss how to stop the racial injustice that was sweeping the country. About sixty people attended, both white and Black— including W. E. B. Du Bois, journalist and anti-lynching activist Ida B. Wells-Barnett, and Black suffrage and civil rights activist Mary Church Terrell—and the National Association for the Advancement of Colored People was born. The mission of the NAACP was to "ensure the political, educational, social,

W. E. B. Du Bois

and economic equality of minority group citizens of the United States, and eliminate race prejudice." Further, the organization sought to "remove all barriers of racial discrimination through democratic processes."

In 1910, the group set up a national office in New York City and established a board of directors. That same year, Du Bois, who was the only Black member of the NAACP's original executives, founded *The Crisis*, the organization's official journal, which covered such issues as the war and lynchings; later, he briefly published *The Brownies' Book*, an edition for children that was also the first periodical exclusively created for Black American youth. Three years after its founding, the NAACP had set up branch offices in major cities such as Boston, St. Louis, and Detroit. Its membership grew exponentially, ballooning from nine thousand members in 1917 to ninety thousand just two years later, spread across three hundred branches.

The NAACP would be instrumental in many civil rights lawsuits, such as *Guinn v. United States*, the 1915 case that struck down Oklahoma's anti-Black grandfather clause. The group also fought to ban *The Birth of a Nation*, the racist film that praised the Ku Klux Klan and inspired its resurgence. About the film, NAACP national secretary May Childs Nerney, who was white, wrote: "If it goes unchallenged it will take years to overcome the harm it is doing. The entire country will acquiesce in the Southern program of segregation, disenfranchisement, and lynching."

When World War I ended in 1918, millions of soldiers returned to the United States, and many white veterans were angry and resentful to find Black Americans were now working the jobs they'd left behind. White people were also concerned that Black veterans, who'd been treated as valued members of their country while fighting in the war, would become "uppity" and start demanding the sort of rights and respect they'd been fighting for abroad.

They were also scared of the guns.

Black gun ownership in the United States already had a long, complicated history by the end of the First World War. Black Civil War veterans who fought for the Union army were allowed to take their rifles home with them when they were discharged; even Black people who hadn't fought in the war could purchase firearms in the North. They used these weapons to defend themselves against infringement on their lives and rights; as one Louisiana freedman said, "As one of the disenfranchised race, I would say to every colored soldier, 'Bring your gun home.'" And the Freedmen's Bureau Act of 1866 allowed formerly enslaved people "to have full and equal benefit of all laws and proceedings concerning personal liberty, [and] personal security . . . including the constitutional right to bear arms." All of this made white people nervous.

Remember the Black codes, the collection of laws that preceded Jim Crow in the post–Civil War period? They were often used to prevent Black people from owning guns in states such as Alabama, Florida, Kentucky, Louisiana, and Mississippi. One Florida law stated that any Black person found with a "bowie knife, dirk, sword, firearms, or ammunition of any kind" could be publicly whipped as punishment. And when Black Civil War veterans returned to their homes in the South, some were met at the train station by public officials, who demanded they turn over their guns. The veterans' punishment if they didn't comply? They could be beaten or shot by law enforcement.

Unsurprisingly, government and law enforcement agents weren't the only ones who attempted to enforce these racist policies. The KKK and other groups of vigilantes took it upon themselves to ride through Black communities and snatch up any guns they found. White mob attacks on Black people in Memphis in 1866, as well as multiple attacks and two murders in Kentucky in 1868, were blamed on Black gun ownership and the mere presence of Black veterans, respectively. Throughout the late 1800s, Black soldiers from Montana to Georgia were terrorized, shot, and lynched, sometimes while wearing their uniforms. And as the white people who perpetrated these crimes faced no consequences, the violence continued into the next century.

In August 1917, Senator James K. Vardaman of Mississippi cautioned his Senate colleagues about Black soldiers returning from World War I: "Impress the Negro with the fact that he is defending the flag, inflate his untutored soul with military airs, teach him that it is his duty to keep the emblem of the nation flying triumphantly in the air—it is but a short step to the conclusion that his political rights must be respected."

Not only did white people believe that Black veterans would start an unwelcome trend by demanding equal treatment once they were back home, they feared specifically that they would use their guns to rebel against the injustices faced each day in the United States. Further, white Americans were still hung up on the idea of protecting white women from Black men, and when they heard about Black soldiers' dalliances with French women overseas, they believed these same men would now feel entitled to sexual relationships with white women in the South. And in 1919, as race riots surged across the country, Black World War I veterans were particular targets for attacks and lynchings, including in Dadeville, Alabama; Waxahachie, Texas; Tyler Station, Kentucky; Pace, Florida; Franklinton, North Carolina; Bogalusa, Louisiana; and various parts of Arkansas and Mississippi.

In April of that year, twenty-four-year-old veteran Daniel Mack of Sylvester, Georgia, accidentally brushed against a white man, which sparked a confrontation; Mack was arrested.

"I fought for you in France to make the world safe for democracy," Mack said during his court hearing. "I don't think you treated me right in putting me in jail and keeping me there, because I've got as much right as anybody else to walk on the sidewalk."

The judge responded, "This is a white man's country and

you don't want to forget it." He then sentenced Mack to thirty days working on a chain gang, wherein groups of prisoners were shackled together and forced to perform hard manual labor, such as ditchdigging, construction, and farming.

Mack had served only a few days of his sentence when a small group of armed white men stormed the jail and kidnapped him, beat and stripped him naked, and left him on the edge of town to die. Miraculously, Mack survived the vicious attack and was later able to leave the South—but he was one of the lucky few. Despite the NAACP's protests in several of these situations, the white mobs were never investigated, and no one was ever taken to trial for their crimes.

Black veterans could even be punished by the military if they dared to speak up about the injustice they encountered. Sergeant Henry Johnson, a Harlem Hellfighter who was one of the first Americans to receive France's Croix de Guerre avec Palme, the highest award for valor given by the French, spoke out against racism and violence toward Black veterans in 1919. Afterward, he was discharged from the army; they withheld his disability pay, although one of his feet was badly injured, and he received no pension. He died impoverished ten years later, at the age of thirty-two.

In May 1919, W. E. B. Du Bois wrote an article entitled "Returning Soldiers" for the NAACP's *The Crisis*. In the piece, he criticized the United States for sending men to fight for democracy overseas that wasn't being practiced at home, writing: "Today we return! We return from the slavery of uniform which the world's madness demanded us to don to the freedom of civil garb. We stand again to look America squarely in the face and call a spade a spade. We sing: This country of ours, despite all its better souls have done and dreamed, is yet a shameful land . . . It *lynches* . . . It *disfranchises* its own citizens . . . It encourages *ignorance* . . . It *steals* from us . . . It *insults* us."

About half a million Black Southerners had migrated to Northern cities by the summer of 1919, and racial tensions were running high. Statistics from the Archives at Tuskegee Institute show racial violence was growing rapidly: lynchings of Black Americans increased from sixty in 1918 to seventy-six just a year later, in 1919. According to the Equal Justice Initiative, at least thirteen veterans were lynched after the Great War.

July Fourth of 1919 was supposed to be a time of celebration; after all, the war was over, the Allies had won, and the soldiers were home. However, as the United States was celebrating the anniversary of its independence from Great Britain, more racial violence would erupt in the nation's capital just weeks later.

On July 19, a nineteen-year-old white woman had been walking home from her job at the Bureau of Engraving and Printing when, she claimed, she was accosted by two Black men. According to the woman, they tried to steal her umbrella and she fended them off until she was saved by a group of white men. Washington, DC, police brought in a Black man named Charles Ralls for questioning, and released him afterward. However, the woman's husband, a naval aviation corps employee, decided on his own that Ralls was guilty. He assembled a mob of more than one hundred servicemen and walked to Bloodfield, a poor Black neighborhood. There, they assaulted Ralls, his wife, and their neighbors. But that wasn't enough for them. Over the next four days, the mob viciously attacked any Black people they could find, concentrating their attacks in the predominantly Black communities of LeDroit Park (by the historically Black institution Howard University), the Seventh Street corridor, and the U Street district.

About a week later, on the South Side of Chicago, Black teenager Eugene Williams was relaxing on a raft in Lake Michigan when he accidentally floated over to the "white side" of the unofficially segregated Twenty-Ninth Street Beach. In response, a white man began pelting him with stones. He struck the seventeen-year-old, who fell into the lake and drowned. Though many Black beachgoers pointed out the man responsible for Williams's death, Chicago police refused to arrest him. Angry with the injustice, crowds began to gather; one Black person shot a gun into the crowd of police and was instantly killed. The race riot that ensued lasted a week, leaving thirty-eight people dead: twenty-three Black, fifteen white. Hundreds more were injured. Once again, fire was employed as a weapon by the white mobs. About a thousand Black people's homes were burned to the ground.

George Haynes, a Black statistician who worked with the US Department of Labor, recorded nearly forty race riots for the year 1919, highlighting the brutally racist violence in such cities as Omaha, Nebraska, and Charleston, South Carolina. But the deadliest riot that year occurred in Elaine, Arkansas.

After slavery was abolished, and landowners in the South could no longer depend on the free labor of enslaved Black people, they had to figure out how to continue producing and harvesting crops. Many of them hired freed Black people as part of a practice called sharecropping, in which the Black laborers worked the land in exchange for a portion of the crops. Sometimes the landowner provided the sharecroppers with housing, along with tools and seed to work the land. However, the workers often had to buy food and other supplies on credit, and many sharecroppers were exploited by the landowners, forced into accepting unfair payments and disproportionate shares of the harvest.

By 1919, sharecropping was still common in Southern states, and that year, Black sharecroppers in Elaine (pronounced by locals with emphasis on the first syllable) wanted to be paid more for their crops. On September 30, they gathered at a church in Hoop Spur, also located in Phillips County, just three miles away, for a meeting of the Progressive Farmers and Household Union of America. Labor unions weren't exactly popular with employers, as they used their collective leverage to demand fair treatment and wages for their members. The Progressive Farmers knew that as a Black union, they'd be considered even more of a threat to the white landowners, so they assigned men with guns to stand guard at the meeting.

At eleven o'clock that evening, a group of white men approached the church and fired shots into the group gathered there. The guards returned the shots, which ended up killing one of the white men and wounding the county's deputy sheriff, also white. Word spread to other towns about the shootout, along with the false accusation that Black people were planning an uprising against white people in Phillips County.

The Arkansas governor called in hundreds of troops from Camp Pike, near Little Rock, to "round up" the "heavily armed" Black people. They arrived on October 2, and, along with a white mob of local residents, estimated to be as large as one thousand, they murdered at least two hundred Black men, women, and children (the number is likely higher and has never been confirmed). The death toll included four brothers—a World War I veteran and his siblings—who'd been on a hunting trip and were forced from a train and shot dead. Yet again, homes were burned and destroyed.

On October 7, the troops were withdrawn and many Black people were jailed for allegedly planning the "insurrection"; on October 31, 122 of them were indicted for a variety of charges, including murder. A dozen men, known as the Elaine Twelve, were convicted of murder and sentenced to death by the all-white jury.

The NAACP soon began fighting the sentence, a fight that would last five long years. After several retrials, appeals, and an appearance before the US Supreme Court, the Elaine Twelve were released. The last of the twelve men was set free on January 14, 1925.

Although the nearly forty race riots of 1919 occurred in different pockets of the country and involved different people, one thing unites them all: fear. The white people who disenfranchised their Black neighbors, who oppressed and persecuted Black World War I veterans, who accused Black men and women of crimes and formed mobs to enact violent revenge, were afraid. Afraid of change, afraid of loss, and, perhaps most of all, afraid of equality.

It was this same fear that soon spread to Tulsa, Oklahoma, planting the seeds for the Greenwood massacre.

The day is just beginning. Sweet-throated birds warble their songs of joy in the treetops, fanned by the refreshing zephyr, and the dew sparkles upon the grass like countless little diamonds. . . . An unbroken stream of pedestrians—male and female—passes down Greenwood Avenue. It is made up of laborers, some empty-handed and others with dinner pails, on their way to work. They hurry along as if they are late. A few of the more pretentious ones pass in their own cars, or in jitneys, or upon buses. Then comes a lull—a lull before the storm.

—B. C. Franklin,
Tulsa Race Massacre survivor

May 31, 1921

Dick Rowland had fled to the home of his mother, Damie, immediately after the elevator incident on May 30. The police didn't seem to be in a hurry to arrest him, though. They didn't send out a bulletin to alert the Tulsa Police Department of the incident, nor did they show up at Damie Ford's boardinghouse that evening. Rowland spent a quiet, anxious night in, waiting for officers who would never come.

But the next morning, the day after Memorial Day, he must have been convinced he was free and clear, or else he wasn't afraid to press his luck. He left the boardinghouse and was soon arrested on Greenwood Avenue by a pair of officers. One of them, Henry C. Pack, was Black—one of the few African American men on the Tulsa police force, which employed about seventy-five officers.

They took Rowland down to the police station to charge him. It was at this point that people began to talk; the town quickly learned that Rowland was in jail, and what his alleged crime was. He had only been in custody for a few hours when law enforcement began to receive death threats aimed at Rowland. The Tulsa police transferred him to the Tulsa County Courthouse on Sixth Street and Boulder Avenue, where he would remain locked up in a jail cell on the top floor of the building.

Although he'd been moved to what was supposed to be safer and more secure conditions, Tulsans knew what could very well be in store for Rowland. As newspaper editor A. J. Smitherman had written in the *Tulsa Star*, "The lynching of Roy Belton explodes the theory that a prisoner is safe on the top of the Court House from mob violence."

The white newspapers also got ahold of this information, which quickly set things into motion. The *Tulsa World* was a morning paper; it hadn't been able to report on the May 30 incident in the Drexel Building the prior day, and its May 31 issue was printed before Rowland's arrest that morning. But the story came through at precisely the perfect time for the afternoon paper the *Tulsa Tribune* to print the news—and an inflammatory front-page headline to go with it:

NAB NEGRO FOR ATTACKING GIRL IN AN ELEVATOR

A negro delivery boy who gave his name to the public as "Diamond Dick" but who has been identified as Dick Rowland, was arrested on South Greenwood avenue this morning by Officers Carmichael and Pack, charged with attempting to assault the 17-year-old white elevator girl in the Drexel building early yesterday.

He will be tried in municipal court this afternoon on a state charge.

The girl said she noticed the negro a few minutes before the attempted assault looking up and down the hallway on the third floor of the Drexel building as if to see if there was anyone in sight but thought nothing of it at the time.

A few minutes later he entered the elevator she claimed, and attacked her, scratching her hands and face and tearing her clothes. Her screams brought a clerk from Renberg's store to her assistance and the negro fled. He was captured and identified this morning both by the girl and the clerk, police say.

Tenants of the Drexel building said the girl is an orphan who works as an elevator operator to pay her way through business college.

Though several people saw that afternoon's *Tribune* in its entirety, no complete physical copies of the May 31 afternoon edition exist. However, several witnesses recalled the headline of the editorial, which is said to have stated:

TO LYNCH NEGRO TONIGHT

That stark headline and the now missing editorial that followed were certainly enough to incite a lynch mob. Word swept quickly throughout both the Black and white sides of Tulsa. The *Tribune* had barely been out for an hour before the rumblings about an impending lynching grew so loud that police and fire commissioner J. M. Adkison called Sheriff Willard McCullough to tell him what was going on.

At around six or seven o'clock that evening, white Tulsans attempted to make good on those rumblings, assembling outside the county courthouse; by 7:30 p.m., the horde was about three hundred strong. It was too late for McCullough to discourage the vigilante seekers—they knew Rowland was in a cell on the top floor, and they wanted their way with him. The crowd continued to grow as darkness settled in. They were shouting at Sheriff McCullough: "Let us have the nigger!"

But McCullough was a different sheriff than the one who'd overseen matters during the Roy Belton lynching the year before. He had only recently become the Tulsa County sheriff, after James Woolley was voted out for his failure to stop Belton's lynching—and he was adamant that a mob wouldn't get to the prisoner this time. Once he was informed of the lynching plans, he'd increased security by sending six armed officers to the roof of the courthouse, positioned the rest on the stairs, and disabled the elevator, all of which would essentially prevent any violent mob members who dared to try to break through from making their way to Rowland's cell.

The mob was no fan of Sheriff McCullough's efforts to keep Rowland safe. They booed him as he attempted to calm them down, and three white men soon came forward and commanded him to hand over the prisoner. McCullough refused. Though he knew he and his men were outnumbered, he remained committed to protecting Rowland.

Over in the Greenwood District, students at Booker T. Washington High School were preparing for the senior prom that evening.

Bill Williams, whose parents owned a popular soda fountain/candy shop, an auto garage, and the Williams

Tulsa's Greenwood District in 1921

Dreamland Theatre, was one of those students decorating the building on Archer Street where the dance would be held. But soon, Williams and the other students learned there would be no prom. They were told to abandon the decorations and head home. White Tulsans weren't the only ones who'd seen the *Tribune* that afternoon and heard talk about a lynching. Rumors were circulating: there was going to be trouble from white people that evening.

But before he went home, Williams decided to stop at his family's movie theater on Greenwood Avenue to check in with his mother, Loula. Once he arrived, he found a group gathered inside, trying to figure out what to do about the white mob that had begun to assemble outside the courthouse.

"We're not going to let this happen," a man said from the stage. "We're going to go downtown and stop this lynching. Close this place down."

Black Tulsans gathered along busy Greenwood Avenue close to where it met with Archer Street. Nearby at the *Tulsa Star* offices, editor A. J. Smitherman held a meeting, a group of Black men that included prominent Greenwood businessman J. B. Stradford, other local leaders, and war veterans. They were trying to decide the best course of action. No Black person had ever been lynched in Tulsa. There was a close call in March 1919, when three Black Tulsans were locked up for the alleged murder of a white ironworker and rumors began to swirl that they would be lynched—but those rumors never turned into fact, as they had with Roy Belton nine months earlier. And the men in Greenwood were determined not to let it happen that evening, either.

Of course, not everyone was on board with the plan to confront the white mob, including Greenwood cofounder O. W. Gurley, who thought his neighbors were heading into a fight they couldn't win. He said the leader of the group, a World War I veteran, "came back from France with exaggerated ideas of equality." But that didn't stop the men who believed it was the best and most necessary course of action. Roy Belton had been lynched after being dragged from that very courthouse—and he was white. The men felt Rowland was in even more danger, and they had to stand up for him and the Black community before it was too late.

Meanwhile, Greenwood resident Barney Cleaver had been telephoning Sheriff McCullough ever since the rumors started. Cleaver, the first Black police officer in Tulsa, had been promoted to deputy sheriff by 1921 and was somewhat of a liaison between the Black community and white law enforcement. He knew the men in Greenwood were planning to go down to where the mob was gathered and reportedly tried to talk them out of it, to no avail. He was trying to get a grasp on what was happening at the courthouse and offered to come down to help keep order. At first, Sheriff McCullough turned down Deputy Sheriff Cleaver's offer of assistance but eventually agreed that he could join him downtown.

Around nine that evening, about twenty-five Black men—including John Williams, Bill's father and Loula's husband—armed themselves with shotguns and rifles and drove over to the courthouse. They headed up the steps and announced they were there to protect the jail. The police

officers on the scene told them they had things under control—
that Rowland was safe and they could go home. However, that
bold offer of protection further riled up the white mob, which
had grown to more than a thousand people by that point. Once
they saw armed Black men—a sight they'd consider a challenge
any other day but particularly so under the circumstances—
the enraged mob sought to arm themselves, as well. Some went
home to get their own guns, while others headed over to the
National Guard armory at Sixth Street and Norfolk Avenue.
Their plan? To break in and steal rifles and ammunition.

Major James A. Bell, a local National Guard officer, had
smelled trouble, however, and already arranged for guardsmen
to meet down at the armory in case their services were needed.
"I went to the front of the building near the southwest corner
where I saw a mob of white men about three or four hundred
strong," Major Bell later recalled. "I explained to them that they
could not get anything here. Someone shouted, 'We don't know
about that, we guess we can.'"

The National Guard fought off the insistent crowd, but not
without repeated attempts by the mob to get their hands on
guns and ammo. Major Bell said the armed guard was able to
break up the mob at the armory "by maintaining a firm stand."

Just a half hour after the couple dozen Black men had been
turned away at the courthouse, the mob had nearly doubled in
size, to two thousand people. By this time, there was no reasoning with them; they ignored pleas from local leaders to disperse.
Police chief John Gustafson, the same chief who had let another
angry mob kidnap and lynch Roy Belton the previous year, was

no help; he failed to call in additional assistance from the police force and didn't bother to stick around to help fend off the mob. Instead, he had returned to police headquarters by the time the crowd grew out of control.

Back in Greenwood, the Black community was still anxiously awaiting news of what was happening at the courthouse, and though the first group of men who'd offered to guard the jail had been told to return home, that didn't stop others from trying their luck. Several small groups headed downtown in cars, making sure people who were out and about could see that they were armed. They wanted to make clear that they were serious about preventing the lynching of Rowland and that they would not be intimidated.

Shortly after 10:00 p.m., a group of seventy-five Black men, triple the size of the first group, drove down to the courthouse with their guns. For a second time, they offered to help the police officers guard the jail, and for a second time, their services were rejected. Deputy Sheriff Barney Cleaver was stationed at the courthouse by this time, urging his neighbors to head back home to Greenwood. Some say of these crucial moments before the massacre began that white people saw armed Black men not only as a general threat, but as an indication that they were starting a "Negro uprising." This put the mob even more on edge, and as the Black men were leaving the courthouse, there was an altercation between a white man and a Black veteran, who held the gun he'd brought home from World War I.

"Nigger, what are you going to do with that pistol?" the white man demanded, stepping to him.

"I'm going to use it if I need to," the Black veteran responded.
"No, you give it to me."

"Like hell I will."

The white man attempted to grab the gun, a shot rang out, and, according to Sheriff McCullough, "the race war was on, and I was powerless to stop it." Whether he truly didn't have the ability to stop what happened next is debatable, but McCullough was right about one thing: this was just the beginning.

A shootout ensued between the Black men and the white mob, reportedly leaving possibly a dozen people, Black and white, wounded or dead. The Black men had every intention of standing their ground and defending themselves, but they were vastly outnumbered at that point—by more than twenty to one. They began retreating back toward Greenwood, with members of the mob hot on their heels, guns loaded and ready. According to a white bystander, "A great many of [the people] lining the sidewalks were holding a rifle or shotgun in one hand, and grasping the neck of a liquor bottle with the other. Some had pistols stuck into their belts."

While this was a dangerous situation in itself, the Tulsa police force was about to make things a whole lot worse. A significant portion of the white mob had moved to the police headquarters on Second Street, where anywhere between four hundred and five hundred men were sworn in as "special deputies." There were no background checks, and no prior law enforcement experience was necessary. The only requirement was to be a white man who wanted to exact "revenge." Deputizing these men was a cover for the white mob—"authorization" they could later use as an excuse for the violence that was about to ensue. The Tulsa police gave the men badges and ribbons to validate their new roles, and, in some cases, the civilians were told in no uncertain terms to go out and kill Black people.

The tone had been set. Members of the white mob without government-issued firearms began looting stores and pawnshops for guns and ammunition. According to one report, a Tulsa police officer handed out guns stolen from a sporting goods store across from police headquarters.

Black people who had happened to be downtown that evening were some of the first victims of the mob. They were shot on sight. A white teenager named William "Choc" Phillips, who would grow up to become a Tulsa police officer, witnessed the violence at the Royal Theater that evening. A Black man who'd been chased by the white mob burst into the theater, looking for a place to hide, and accidentally ended up onstage in front of the film that was playing. "One of [the men from the mob] saw the Negro and yelled, 'There he is, heading for the aisle,'" Phillips recalled. "As he finished the sentence, a roaring blast from a shotgun dropped the Negro man by the end of the orchestra pit."

Although a smaller crowd had returned to the courthouse amid all the chaos, demanding "Bring the rope!" and "Get the nigger!," their cries were not backed up by force. This was no longer about Dick Rowland and his alleged crime.

War had been declared on any and every Black person in Tulsa.

I was too young to personally remember details of the riot, but I heard my parents talk about the riot—how bad it was, how it destroyed so much property that Blacks had worked so hard to acquire.

—Delois Vaden Ramsey,
Tulsa Race Massacre survivor

4

Black Wall Street Comes Alive

There would have been no Greenwood District without a man named O. W. Gurley.

The child of a formerly enslaved couple, Ottowa W. Gurley was born in Huntsville, Alabama, on December 25, 1868. When he was eight years old, he moved with his family to the majority-Black town of Pine Bluff, Arkansas, where he attended public schools but was primarily self-educated. Gurley graduated from Pine Bluff's Branch Normal College, an institution founded to train Black educators to teach at Black schools within segregated Arkansas.

In addition to teaching, Gurley held a job with the United States Postal Service. He also worked in a position appointed by President Grover Cleveland, though the details of what exactly that position entailed have been lost to history. Gurley resigned from this job in 1888 for better opportunities; he wanted to leave the South, as he felt he would never be able to achieve his goals for success there, given the color of his skin. He married a woman named Emma Evans, and together they traveled from Arkansas to Oklahoma to try to secure land during the era of the famous land runs.

In September 1893, Gurley participated in the Cherokee Strip, or Cherokee Outlet opening, which was the fourth and largest of the land runs, with more than 100,000 people partaking from all over the United States and even other countries. Gurley was serious about creating new opportunities for himself, and he ran fifty miles before he claimed land in what would become the town of Perry, Oklahoma.

O.W. and Emma settled in nicely in their new town, which was about eighty miles outside of Tulsa. With his background in education, Gurley was well-suited to his appointment as superintendent of the town's schools. Later, he opened a general store, which he operated for the next ten years. But despite his success in Perry, Gurley wanted to move on to bigger and better things. More specifically: oil. The oil boom in Tulsa had begun, and like many entrepreneurs at the time, Gurley was looking to capitalize on it. He sold his store and purchased forty acres of land on the north side of Tulsa's Frisco railroad tracks, where he and Emma moved in 1906.

Gurley had a plan for the neighborhood from the moment he moved there. He wanted to build a community where other ambitious, "upwardly mobile" Black people could put down roots, and he rightfully anticipated that freedmen and people who longed to escape the South, like him, would migrate to Tulsa. Sure enough, Tulsa soon became known as the oil capital of the world, and thousands of people were moving to the area for new opportunities—including Black Americans. Though it wasn't easy for Black people to secure jobs in the oil fields, they knew they'd be able to find work in service jobs for the influx of Tulsa residents, such as housekeeping, groundskeeping, and working in restaurants.

Gurley's first business was a grocery store; he built it on a street he called Greenwood Avenue, which got its name from a town in Mississippi. Gurley's vision for this new Black community was vivid from the start: he separated his land into lots for both businesses and housing before any of it had been built. However, although he was an enterprising businessman, Gurley didn't develop Greenwood all by himself. Shortly after he and his wife moved to Tulsa, he met a like-minded man named J. B. Stradford.

Stradford's father, J.C., had been enslaved, gaining his freedom when he escaped to Stratford, Ontario, and worked to raise money to legally free himself and his family. J.C., short for Julius Caesar, likely changed his family's last name to a version of this town's name to commemorate their freedom, and because the family that had enslaved him had never given him a last name—not even the slaveholder's surname, which was custom. His son J.B., short for John the Baptist, was born in 1861, the same year the American Civil War began.

Not much is known about his childhood, but J. B. Stradford

began making his ambitions known from a young age. He earned an undergraduate degree from Oberlin College—where he met his wife, Augusta—and a law degree from Indiana University. After he completed his education, Stradford and Augusta moved around the Midwest and the South, where they opened various businesses, such as boardinghouses, pool halls, and shoeshine parlors. In 1899, they moved to Tulsa, and Stradford began working informally with O. W. Gurley to build up a prosperous Black community.

Both Gurley and Stradford owned eponymous boardinghouses on Greenwood Avenue, with Stradford's property claiming the title of the largest Black-owned hotel in the country at the time. The Stradford Hotel boasted fifty-four rooms, along with a restaurant, a saloon, a pool hall, and a place to gamble. Stradford spared no expense, as he wanted his hotel to rival the lodging for white people across the train tracks in Tulsa. By today's standards, the property would be valued at $2.5 million.

Though his focus was local, building up Greenwood with Gurley, Stradford never lost sight of the broader fight for racial equality. In December 1908, J.B. and Augusta were arrested for disobeying Jim Crow laws when they refused to ride in the Black railroad car on a train headed from Kansas to Bartlesville. They were snatched off the train and arrested in Bartlesville, per a report in Kansas's *Iola Daily Index*, which also stated that Stradford and his daughter had been arrested on similar charges the previous year. Eight years later, Stradford relentlessly fought a Tulsa city ordinance that blatantly enforced housing segregation;

he led a protest of hundreds at Greenwood's Dreamland Theatre and petitioned the Tulsa mayor, though the law was upheld
even after the Oklahoma Supreme Court overturned the ordinance the next year. Stradford, an attorney by training, also
worked to prevent lynchings by representing potential victims
in court and gathering with other armed Black men to intimidate white mobs.

Meanwhile, Gurley and Stradford continued to grow
Greenwood. In addition to rental properties, Gurley operated
his grocery store, started an employment agency, and built a
Masonic lodge. He was eventually named a sheriff's deputy,
with the primary task of overseeing the city's Black residents.
Gurley and Stradford were also heavily invested in the real
estate business, buying and selling land and loaning money to
entrepreneurs like themselves, who helped develop Greenwood.
While some white people owned land in the district, the focus
was on building up and supporting Black businesses and professionals.

These Black business owners came from a variety of back-
grounds: Some had been born into slavery in the South, or had
been formerly enslaved by citizens of the Native Nations forced
to relocate to Indian Territory, but the majority of Greenwood's
residents had sought out Tulsa as a place of promise, during the
beginning of its oil boom in the early twentieth century. Some
of them had made stops in Oklahoma's smaller towns, including
some of the all-Black communities, where they gained experience creating and building their own businesses, then brought
that entrepreneurship to Greenwood.

Emma Buckner's sewing shop, located at 1120 N. Hartford Avenue, photographed shortly before it was burned down by the white mob

By 1921, Greenwood was home to a Black hospital, a Black public library, two Black schools, two Black newspapers, two theaters, three fraternal organizations, five hotels, eleven boardinghouses, and about a dozen churches. The main intersection was Greenwood Avenue and Archer Street, which was a block away from the railroad tracks that served as the line between Black and white Tulsa. Greenwood Avenue extended north for more than a mile, and it was unique: while other streets in Tulsa ran through both the Black and white neighborhoods, the titular avenue started just north of the Frisco railroad tracks and did not spill into the white areas of town.

The commercial district, known as Deep Greenwood, consisted of several blocks that included the southern end of Greenwood Avenue and its side streets. Lined with redbrick buildings, some of which stretched to three stories, one could find just about anything they needed in Deep Greenwood, with reportedly six hundred businesses within its thirty-five city blocks by 1921. You could shop at Elliott & Hooker's Clothing Emporium at 124 North Greenwood, then cross the street for tailoring at H. L. Byars's shop; Hope Watson's dry cleaning business was conveniently located at 322 Archer Street, just around the corner. William Anderson was the neighborhood jeweler, while Henry Lilly's shop was there for all your upholstery needs. And anyone who needed to have professional photos taken could visit A. S. Newkirk's studio. Black businesses continued to pop up in the rapidly expanding community, including a roller-skating rink, more grocery stores, a post office substation, women's clubs, and a YMCA.

Food, which has always been a significant aspect of Black culture, was an important part of Greenwood, too. People gathered at barbecue joints, sandwich shops, or the Little Café, where they "lined up waiting for their specialty—chicken or smothered steak with rice and brown gravy." Rolly Huff, Greenwood's first portable ice cream vendor, owned a confectionery with his wife, Ada, on Archer Street between Detroit and Cincinnati Avenues, where they served customers cold drinks such as Coca-Cola and sarsaparilla, a root beer–like soda. Doc's Beanery and Hamburger Kelly's were popular places to grab a bite, and if you were in the mood for a home-cooked meal at

2:00 a.m., Lilly Johnson's Liberty Café was the late-night spot to hit up.

The headquarters and printing press for A. J. Smitherman's *Tulsa Star* newspaper were located in Greenwood. Simon Berry, described by historian Eddie Faye Gates as "colorful, flamboyant," and "a smooth talker," owned a transportation company that ferried Greenwood residents across town in Ford Model T cars and buses, and eventually chartered airplanes for the wealthy oil executives in the area. It has been said that Berry's company was a model for the city's modern-day Tulsa Transit service.

Beauty parlors and barbershops have long been a staple of the Black community, and Greenwood was no exception. Mabel Little owned Little Rose Beauty Salon, located in Deep Greenwood, which she established in 1915 after years of working as a motel housekeeper. She'd learned everything she knew about cutting and styling hair from her aunt, and later earned a certification from the beauty course of Madam C. J. Walker, "the first Black woman millionaire in America." Customers would visit Little's beauty shop to get their hair washed, straightened, or fashioned into the popular styles of the time. Thursday nights were particularly busy for Little; known as "Maid's Night Out," this was when the young domestic workers would leave the white neighborhoods and head to Greenwood for a night out on the town.

John and Loula Williams, who'd moved to Oklahoma from Mississippi in the early 1900s, owned an auto repair shop, as well as the three-story Williams Building on the northwest corner of

Greenwood Avenue and Archer Street. They lived on the second floor of the building and rented the top floor to doctors, lawyers, and dentists for office space. The first floor housed a confectionery, which sold candy and ice cream, had a fancy soda fountain, and seated almost fifty people. The couple also opened the first Black movie theater in the city of Tulsa: spearheaded by Loula, the Williams Dreamland Theatre opened in 1914 on Greenwood Avenue. Its showings included a roster of silent films, as well as live musical shows and revues, which were a mix of singing, dancing, monologues, and skits. With seating for 750 people, it was Tulsa's second-largest movie theater, after the white-owned Dixie Theater across the street, which seated a thousand. The Williamses were also the first Black family in Tulsa to own an automobile, a sign of prestige at the time.

When Loula and John's son, Bill, had asked his father why they'd moved to Oklahoma, John responded, "Well, I came out to the promised land." Indeed, Greenwood was beginning to resemble neighborhoods in big cities like Chicago and New York, with its doctors and attorneys, theaters and restaurants, booming real estate market, and millionaires in the making.

Thursday nights and Sundays after church were the busiest times in Deep Greenwood. The Black Tulsans who lived in white neighborhoods because of their jobs happily traveled to Greenwood on their days off, whether to see a movie, visit friends and family, attend church, or patronize one of the many businesses in the commercial district. The housing conditions of those who did live in Greenwood varied; while plenty of Black Tulsans owned nice homes along Detroit Avenue and other streets in the district—some were said to have accrued more than $100,000 in assets—others were confined to flimsy homes and shacks on the side streets off Greenwood Avenue.

Despite this discrepancy, it cannot be overstated how unique Greenwood was among Black communities nationwide. While Black people were still being disenfranchised in the Southern states from which many Greenwood residents had migrated, Greenwood was absolutely thriving. The community's focus on businesses that were Black-owned, Black-operated, and patronized primarily by Black people meant that each dollar spent in Greenwood would circulate throughout the businesses and people there around thirty times; the wealth stayed in the community and continued to grow it.

But Black Wall Street, as it would come to be called, wasn't just about for-profit businesses and institutions. Greenwood was also home to several churches; the district contained more churches than the white community did, on a per capita basis. In addition to Sunday church services, Black Tulsans attended Bible study or meetings of national religious societies throughout the week, and Black teenagers joined youth groups. The list of more than a dozen Black churches included several denominations, such as Bethel Seventh Day Adventist, Brown's Chapel, Church of God, Church of God in Christ, First Baptist, and Vernon African Methodist Episcopal Church. First organized in 1909, Mount Zion Baptist Church began construction on a new building in 1916, a project that cost $92,000. The beautiful new building on Elgin Avenue was completed five years later and dedicated on April 4, 1921, just two months before Greenwood residents would clash with the white mob in front of the Tulsa courthouse.

With its own hospital in the neighborhood, Greenwood employed fifteen Black doctors. Dr. A. C. Jackson, a venerable physician and surgeon, was undoubtedly the most prominent one. Jackson was born in Memphis, Tennessee, in February 1879, to a formerly enslaved couple. After his father, Civil War veteran Townsend Jackson, was threatened by a white lynch mob for visiting a white tobacco store, the family left town. They moved to Guthrie, Oklahoma, in 1889, shortly after it was established. The Jacksons were a welcome addition to Guthrie, and Townsend was appointed town jailer and elected as justice of the peace. A.C. did well in school and was accepted to Meharry Medical College in Nashville, a historically Black institution. After graduating, he returned to Guthrie and married a woman named Julia. However, the new Jim Crow laws in Oklahoma had changed the racial atmosphere of Guthrie, so the whole family moved to Tulsa in 1912, their sights set on the upwardly mobile Greenwood District.

Dr. A. C. Jackson

Dr. Jackson set up his medical practice on the corner of Greenwood Avenue and Archer Street, quickly gaining a clientele that respected him. In fact, he was so revered that white patients entrusted him with their medical care, too, despite Tulsa's segregated hospitals. He established a second practice in nearby Claremore, Oklahoma, in 1916, and two years later, he was in talks with the Tulsa mayor about opening a Black hospital on the corner of Boston Avenue and Archer Street. Dr. Jackson eventually became president of the Oklahoma State Medical Association, and William and Charles Mayo, who founded the nationally revered Mayo Clinic in Minnesota, called him "the most able Negro surgeon in America."

Greenwood was also home to well-respected attorneys. Buck Colbert "B. C." Franklin had moved to Tulsa in 1921 from the all-Black town of Rentiesville, Oklahoma, where he'd worn many hats, including the town's justice of the peace, the postmaster, the only attorney, and a leading entrepreneur. However, as his son John Hope Franklin later explained, "there was not a decent living in all those activities," which brought Franklin to the oil town of Tulsa with the goal of more profitable and plentiful legal work. He set up a practice there and would later become one of the massacre's most significant figures just months after arriving in Tulsa.

The residents of Greenwood placed great emphasis on education: Booker T. Washington High School was a top-tier institution that prepared students for enrollment at elite, predominantly white schools such as Columbia University and Oberlin College, and prestigious HBCUs (historically Black colleges and universities) like Howard University and Spelman College. Educators were so valued that they earned some of the highest salaries in Greenwood. In fact, famous educator and author Booker T. Washington is responsible for naming the district "Negro Wall Street."

Despite Greenwood's exceptional growth throughout the first two decades of the twentieth century, its success did not go unresented by white Tulsans—or, ultimately, unchallenged.

Black people had created Greenwood out of necessity; owning, operating, and supporting Black businesses was their only path to living the full, unbothered lives that white people were allowed to live while not violating the strict Jim Crow laws that ruled the state. Though not all Black Tulsans resided there—domestic workers performing jobs as housekeepers, drivers, cooks, and butlers often lived in Tulsa's white communities, staying in the servants' quarters of their white employers—by the beginning of 1921, Greenwood had attracted more than ten thousand Black residents, who were homeowners, business owners, and loyal patrons of the community's businesses.

White Tulsans were well aware of what was going on across the railroad tracks—and many of them didn't like it. They felt Black Americans hadn't earned their right to such wealth and success, or to simply be left alone. Jealous of what the Black community had built on their own, some white people referred to Greenwood as "Little Africa." Because of segregation laws and personal choices, many white Tulsans never socialized or interacted with Black Tulsans. They attended all-white churches, worked with all white people, and sent their children to all-white schools. This general ignorance of the lives and personalities of their Black neighbors left substantial room for spreading bigoted rumors and racial stereotypes.

With more people drawn to the growing city, crime had been on the rise in Tulsa over the years. In late April 1921, a federal agent went undercover for five days and subsequently wrote the "Federal Vice Report on Vice Conditions in Tulsa," which criticized the city's gambling, illegal drug use, auto theft, bootlegging of alcohol during Prohibition, burglary, gun violence, and sex work. Vehicle theft was so widespread, apparently, that "a number of companies have canceled all policies on cars in Tulsa." Murder was also a problem; in addition to the Roy Belton lynching, 1920 saw the killing of two on-duty Tulsa police officers. The federal agent's report determined: "Vice conditions in this city are extremely bad."

The high crime rate, combined with racial ignorance, vigilante justice, and a growing intolerance for Black Americans around the country, led to a tension that simmered over the city and was poised to boil over by late May 1921. But jealousy and resentment cannot be overlooked as significant motivators that would lead to the Tulsa Race Massacre that year.

An article published in a 1907 edition of national magazine *The Independent* noted that "the Negro of Indian Territory is also a landowner. The ex-slaves of the Five Tribes are protected in their holdings as are the Indians. . . . In both divisions of the state, there are probably a larger percentage of Negroes who own their own homes and are in comfortable circumstances than elsewhere in the United States." This was just a year after O. W. Gurley had purchased the land that would become the foundation of Tulsa's Greenwood District. White Tulsans were likely unprepared for the great success their Black neighbors across the Frisco train tracks would achieve, and once they saw the gains Black Tulsans had made, they were determined to put a stop to it.

Michelle Place, executive director of the Tulsa Historical Society, told History.com, "I think the word jealousy is certainly appropriate during this time. If you have particularly poor whites who are looking at this prosperous community who have large homes, fine furniture, crystals, china, linens, etc., the reaction is 'they don't deserve that.'"

The phrase "jealousy is the root of all evil" has perhaps never been truer than in the case of white Americans who have viewed successful Black Americans as a threat. And the depths of that evil would soon be exposed in Tulsa, Oklahoma.

I was seven years old when the riot broke out.
Some of the riot survivors my age remember
a lot about the riot. But I just can't remember
much about it. I guess it was so horrible that
my mind has just blotted it out.

—Johnnie L. Grayson Brown,
Tulsa Race Massacre survivor

5

Extra! Extra! Read All About It!, or the Promise of a Lynching

Before logging into social media was part of our daily routine, or the internet and television even existed, newspapers were the primary way people kept up-to-date on the state of the world.

Almost as soon as European colonizers created settlements in what is now the United States, Americans have relied on newspapers for information on political matters and wars, advertisements, editorials, comics, and local, national, and international affairs. The first American newspaper, Boston-based *Publick Occurrences, Both Foreign and Domestick*, was founded in 1690 and intended to be a monthly; it lasted only one issue before the Massachusetts governor shut it down. This was legal at the time, as the free press wasn't established until 1791, with the First Amendment. The nation's first official newspaper, the *Boston News-Letter*, debuted in 1704. It was published as a weekly until 1776, and printed news from London, along with obituaries, politics, and advertisements to purchase enslaved Africans.

These initial publications were unequivocally aimed at a white readership. The newspapers not only ran ads to purchase enslaved people as early as their founding, but they didn't report news or concerns that were useful or of interest to the Black community. In fact, it was quite the opposite; many of them routinely denigrated African Americans, publishing false stories to further support disenfranchisement of the Black race. Black Americans wouldn't see a newspaper that addressed their own community and concerns until the next century, in 1827.

Freedom's Journal, the very first Black-owned and -operated newspaper, launched in March of that year. Founded in New York City the same year the state abolished slavery, the paper was distributed as a four-page weekly by its senior and junior editors, Samuel E. Cornish and John B. Russwurm. Notably, just the year before, Jamaican native Russwurm had become the third Black college graduate ever in the United States. Cornish, who founded the first Black Presbyterian church in New York, and was a founding member of the American Anti-Slavery Society, would go on to be called "the most important Black journalist before Frederick Douglass." The paper covered news from regional, national, and international perspectives with the mission of improving life for the more than quarter of a million freed Black people in the North.

The first issue included a note underscoring the paper's

purpose to give its readership a voice that had been denied to them since the founding of the country: "Too long have others spoken for us. Too long has the publick been deceived by misrepresentations, in things which concern us dearly . . ."

While *Freedom's Journal* primarily covered issues relevant to Black Americans—it argued in support of the Black vote and condemned slavery—it also published articles about African countries, such as Sierra Leone, and those in the diaspora, like Haiti. Among all this news, readers could also find biographies of well-known Black people; announcements for births, deaths, and weddings; and listings for jobs and housing. *Freedom's Journal* soon became so popular that circulation expanded from New York to ten more states; Washington, DC; Canada; Haiti; and Europe. Six months after the paper published its first issue, Cornish resigned and Russwurm became the lone editor. Upon Cornish's departure, the paper began to embrace the American Colonization Society, a primarily white organization that favored sending freed Black Americans to the African country of Liberia. Readers didn't appreciate the shift, and the paper lasted only two years in total, publishing its final issue in March 1829. After Russwurm moved to Liberia, where he remained until his death in 1851, Cornish tried to resurrect *Freedom's Journal* under a new name, but it was unsuccessful.

Freedom's Journal's life was short, but it paved the way for hundreds of other Black-owned and -operated newspapers, some of which still exist today. By the time the American Civil War began in 1861, more than forty of them had been launched in the United States.

The American Colonization Society

In December 1816, Reverend Robert Finley of the Presbyterian Church founded the American Colonization Society (ACS). The intention was to help freed Black people reach their full potential and spread the beliefs of Christianity—in Africa. In Finley's view, Black Americans would lead better lives in "the land of their fathers," despite the fact that many of them had been born in the United States and never visited an African country. He also believed that sending Black people there would eventually help abolish slavery.

Though it seems on the surface that Finley was looking out for the well-being of Black people, he founded the ACS because of racist beliefs. He and his fellow members, who were mostly white, were more concerned about the lives of white Americans, and felt that free Black people were "unfavorable to [white America's] industry and morals." Finley felt it was more preferable to send an entire race to another continent rather than provide aid to poor Black people or accept interracial marriage.

The ACS—whose members included a nephew of George Washington, as well as Francis Scott Key, who wrote the poem that became the national anthem "The Star-Spangled Banner"—formed an African colony in 1822, which became the country of Liberia in 1847. While most Black people opposed the idea of moving to a country they didn't know, the ACS helped send more than twelve thousand free Black Americans to Liberia by the late 1860s, with funding from local, state, and even the federal government.

Interest in the program declined after the American Civil War, when Black people were emancipated, and the ACS stopped its emigration program, instead focusing on education and spreading Christianity throughout Liberia. The organization disbanded in 1964.

One of Tulsa's first weekly newspapers was the *Indian Republican*, founded in 1893 and descended from the *Indian Chief*, which was first published in 1884 when the area was just a tent city. But businesspeople didn't like the reporting of the *Indian Republican*—they felt the writing style was too sensational. The newspaper engaged in a type of reporting known as "yellow journalism," which manipulated storytelling—and sometimes the truth—to gain more readers. Today, we see this in blogs and on websites centered around questionable gossip or extreme political views that fail to present all the facts.

In 1895, a group of Tulsa residents published the first issue of the weekly *New Era*, which they created to provide a more positive view of their city—and which they hoped would attract more settlers to the area. Three years later, as more people began putting down roots in the city, the *New Era* was renamed the *Tulsa Democrat*. The paper liked to brag on Tulsa's achievements, such as construction of new railroads, cotton gins, and businesses—and its editors were equally passionate about reporting on its neighbors throughout Indian Territory, who they said couldn't keep up with Tulsa's progress. When the paper proved to be unprofitable, the publishers sold it, and the new owner converted the *Tulsa Democrat* to a daily publication. The first issue of the new iteration was printed in September 1904, with the promise of "the upbuilding of Tulsa morally, mentally, and materially." Though the town was primarily Democratic, the paper took a neutral political view, stating "no preference will be shown to one [party] over another."

The *Tulsa Democrat* was sold again just a year later in 1905, coinciding with the founding of Republican newspaper the *Tulsa Daily World*. The *World* was initially focused on promoting a Republican party faction that included a former congressional delegate and Oklahoma Territory's governor. Oklahoma wouldn't become a state for two more years, and the paper supported the two territories combining for single statehood; it also opposed Jim Crow laws. However, from the start, the *Tulsa Democrat*, which was the largest paper at the time, expressed doubt that the competing daily—and the second Republican newspaper in town—would survive, stating: "Outside of a small number of Republican politicians . . . everyone has thought that for the present the newspaper field was filled."

The *Tulsa Democrat* didn't change ownership again for more than a decade, when an oil magnate named Charles Page bought the paper in 1916. Page, who had founded the town of Sand Springs, a suburb west of Tulsa, was not exactly buying the paper out of noble journalistic pursuits. He was engaged in a dispute with competitor the *Tulsa Daily World* about a business transaction and wanted to boost his profile by owning a paper.

However, he soon became tired of the media industry, and three years later, the paper was sold once again, this time to Richard Lloyd Jones.

In contrast to Page, who was known for many roles in his lifetime, including business developer, oilman, and philanthropist, Jones was first and foremost a journalist. He'd been an editor for *Cosmopolitan* (yes, that *Cosmopolitan*) shortly after the turn of the century, then worked as a writer and editor for *Collier's Weekly* for eight years. In 1911, Jones yearned to operate his own paper, so he bought the *Wisconsin State Journal*, becoming the editor and publisher. He edited the paper from Madison, the state's capital, for the next eight years. In 1919, Jones sold the *Journal* and became the new owner of the *Tulsa Democrat*.

Along with a new owner came yet another change: Jones named his new venture the *Tulsa Tribune-Democrat*. He wanted his paper to reflect the spirit of elected tribunes from early Rome, writing: "Like the tribunes of old, the *Tulsa Tribune-Democrat* seeks to be watchful day and night of the political rights and liberties of the people, irrespective of party, race or religion." The first issue was published on December 6, in which Jones wrote an impassioned editorial that clearly laid out the paper's objective: "The function of a newspaper is to SERVE THE PEOPLE. The function of a pamphlet is to serve a party or a propaganda. The *Tulsa Tribune-Democrat* is a newspaper and not a pamphlet." The signed editorial went on to say that while the paper hoped to retain its Democratic readers, "we want to make a newspaper so just and fair and truthful that Republicans will likewise choose to read it. . . . We never want to be so blindly partisan, so oblivious to our own party's deficiencies . . . so encumbered with prejudice that we fail to tell the truth in our news."

Less than a month later, the word *Democrat* was gone, and the paper was simply called the *Tulsa Tribune*. The *Tribune* reported on everything from voter fraud to business scams; Jones even published stories about purported plans to abduct him. And though he had promised to serve the people, to be "fair and truthful" in the *Tribune*, he was no stranger to being called out for his loose relationship with facts. Back when he was editing and publishing the *Wisconsin State Journal*, the nearby *Madison Democrat* accused Jones of employing yellow journalism to attract more readers.

The front page of the *Tulsa Tribune* on June 2, 1921, the day after the massacre

The *Tulsa Star*, the city's first Black-owned newspaper, was founded as a weekly in 1912 by A. J. Smitherman. Originally published as the *Muskogee Star*, the paper's Democratic views contrasted deeply with the primarily Republican mindset among the Black community at the time. The paper shifted to a more frequent publishing schedule in 1913 when the headquarters were moved to Tulsa, and the name was subsequently changed to the *Tulsa Daily Star*.

Though the paper deviated from traditional Black American political views, it focused wholeheartedly on issues that affected the Black community. The *Tulsa Star* was a place for Black Tulsans to see themselves. It ran announcements for graduations, weddings, and anniversaries, along with obituaries, and differentiated itself from white newspapers by actually printing photos of Black Tulsa residents.

Smitherman would become an important figure in the story of the Tulsa Race Massacre, but his own story started in December 1883, when he was born in Alabama. The next decade, the Smitherman family moved to Indian Territory, where A.J. (short for Andrew Jackson) was raised. After attending prestigious universities in Kansas and Illinois, and earning a law degree in Philadelphia, Smitherman married a woman named Ollie. They had five children together.

The conservative stance of the *Tulsa Star* was undoubtedly informed by Smitherman's personal views. He believed in the "pull yourself up by your bootstraps" mentality, meaning he didn't think Black people should accept help from anyone else in the pursuit to not only survive but thrive. He aligned himself with the Democratic Party because he didn't believe Republicans were doing enough to help the Black community.

Once back in Oklahoma, Smitherman used his law degree to fight injustice for citizens of the Native Nations, as well as Africans who were formerly enslaved by citizens of the Native Nations, whose land was in danger of being taken by white settlers due to thin land-ownership laws and racist guardianship regulations. Smitherman was also focused on enfranchising Black people; he set up a precinct for Black voters, where he was also appointed the inspector of elections at a time when Black Americans were often threatened, intimidated, or even killed for trying to vote in the South.

Smitherman took his first newspaper job in 1908, when he began working for the *Muskogee Cimiter*. He gained enough experience after three years to start his own paper, the *Muskogee Star*, which was also focused on Black progress. He was a member of the Western Negro Press Association (later called the Associated Negro Press), and eventually served as president of the organization for nearly a dozen years. In 1917, Smitherman investigated a story about a white mob that burned the homes of about twenty Black families in Dewey, Oklahoma. He submitted his report to the governor and also published his findings in the *Tulsa Star*; both of these actions were responsible for the arrest of thirty-six white people involved in the mob— including the mayor of Dewey.

A year later, Smitherman interfered in two attempted

lynchings in the state, in one instance getting arrested during his effort to save the life of a young Black boy. Smitherman believed that Black people should arm themselves when necessary to protect their community, and he wasn't afraid to say so, whether in person, in a letter, or in his own publication. In fact, in September 1920, shortly after Claude Chandler was lynched under false murder charges in Oklahoma City, Smitherman wrote: "While the boy was in jail, and while there was danger of mob violence, any set of citizens had a legal right—it was their duty—to arm themselves . . . and take a life if need be to uphold the law and protect the prisoner."

Richard Lloyd Jones may have had every intention of changing his journalistic style by the time he took over the *Tribune*, but he certainly broke his own oath to be "fair and truthful" in 1921. No sole entity or person is responsible for the Tulsa Race Massacre; blame can be laid in many directions, and it is shared by many people, laws, and customs of the time. But the *Tulsa Tribune* is in large part to blame for its inflammatory and premature headline that reportedly ran the afternoon before the massacre:

TO LYNCH NEGRO TONIGHT

Historian Scott Ellsworth wrote: "The *Tribune*, through its May 31 issue, was the single most important force in the creation of the lynch mob outside of the courthouse; anything Dick Rowland might have done was secondary."

While several people reported seeing this incendiary headline and the editorial beneath it, to this day no complete copy of the May 31 *Tulsa Tribune* has been found. Archived versions on microfilm show a missing space where it likely would have run, and historians surmise that this was where the editorial was set. But if a copy containing the full editorial exists, no one has come forward to offer it up.

The May 31 article about Dick Rowland with the headline "Nab Negro for Attacking Girl in an Elevator," on the other hand, has survived. The five-paragraph, front-page story used the word *assault*, which may seem ambiguous now but at the time was synonymous with "rape." And nonconsensual relationships were always assumed when a Black man and a white woman were associated. As such, the *Tribune*'s competitor the *Tulsa World* blamed the afternoon paper for instigating violence with the article. The *World* interviewed Tulsa Police Department chief of detectives J. W. Patton, who said the *Tribune*'s "colored and untrue account . . . incited such a racial spirit upon the part of the whites, and under the impression there would be a lynching the armed blacks invaded the business district. If the facts as told the police had only been printed I do not think there would have been any riot whatever."

(To be clear, the *Tulsa World*, while somewhat sympathetic toward Black Tulsans at the time, had its own questionable perspective on race relations when the massacre occurred. Although it printed "the only bylined story about the massacre and its aftermath to appear in either Tulsa daily newspaper" on June 2, in which its reporter Faith Hieronymus interviewed Black people after the events of June 1, the *World* published an editorial two days later with the headline "Bad Niggers." The intent was to persuade the "innocent, hard-working colored element" in Greenwood to keep the people who "boast of being 'bad niggers'" in check. And Hieronymus's story featured a subhead that read "Black, but Human.")

Walter White, an anti-lynching activist and NAACP leader, also blamed the *Tribune*'s front-page article for inciting the Tulsa Race Massacre. "Without pausing to find whether or not the story was true, without bothering with the slight detail of investigating the character of the woman who made the outcry (as a matter of fact, she was of exceedingly doubtful reputation), a mob of 100 percent Americans set forth on a wild rampage," he wrote. (The "100 percent Americans" description is a reference to terminology used by the Ku Klux Klan, which had reemerged in recent years.)

Whether the "To Lynch Negro Tonight" editorial ever existed is still up for debate by some historians. Skeptics believe that, if it had run as witnesses claimed, the *Tulsa World* or Oklahoma City's *Black Dispatch*, run by Black activist Roscoe Dunjee, would likely have mentioned it. Both covered the massacre, and both were openly critical of the *Tulsa Tribune* in those years. But there is no record of either paper mentioning the infamous editorial. And according to the *Tulsa World*, a reward was offered for a copy of the editorial back in 1997, and still no one came forward. While it is surprising that a copy of it has never been found, both Black and white Tulsans reported having read it. And as Tulsans and Oklahomans worked hard in the years following the massacre to hide those eighteen hours of racial terror, it would not be surprising if any existing copies had simply been buried for eternity.

One thing is certain: words matter. With newspapers serving as the primary source of information back in the 1920s, journalists had a great responsibility to report the truth, just as journalists do today. And while many underlying issues led to the Tulsa Race Massacre, the *Tulsa Tribune*'s reckless, sensational, and factually dubious reporting on May 31, 1921, had a tragic effect on the city it represented.

A family friend came from a hotel on Greenwood where he worked and knocked on our door. He was so scared he could not sit still, nor lie down. He just paced up and down the floor talking about the "mess" going on downtown and on Greenwood.

—**Ernestine Gibbs**,
Tulsa Race Massacre survivor

June 1, 1921

By the time the clock struck midnight on June 1, Black Tulsans were officially in danger. It was late. It was dark. But the violence was just beginning.

A white-presenting Black Tulsan had attended the meeting where white men were being sworn in as "special deputies" by the Tulsa Police Department and headed back to Greenwood to share the news. He found his roommate, Seymour Williams, and told him that the white mob was going to attack the Black neighborhood from the west. Williams was a teacher at Booker T. Washington High School—and a Black army veteran who had served in France during World War I. He grabbed his army-issue revolver and hurried over to Greenwood Avenue, where residents had begun to gather.

After explaining what he'd heard, Williams tried to convince his neighbors off Standpipe Hill to come with him to protect the district. But "not a damn one" would join him, so he ended up guarding the area to the west of Greenwood by himself.

By this time, Black people and white people were firing guns at one another across the Frisco railroad tracks that separated the two communities, a shootout that lasted about an hour and a half. Then, not content with the damage they'd already done downtown, white people set off in their cars toward Greenwood, randomly shooting into the homes of Black Tulsans. They began breaking into houses, murdering people at close range.

At 10:14 p.m., Major Byron Kirkpatrick of the Tulsa National Guard had called Adjutant General Charles F. Barrett of the state National Guard in Oklahoma City to tell him things were getting bad, but he didn't receive word that they were sending anyone. Now, just past 12:30 a.m., Major Kirkpatrick called Oklahoma City again to report things were not improving and perhaps would get even worse if they did not send help immediately. Governor J. B. A. Robertson told him to draw up a request for help signed by Police Chief Gustafson, Sheriff McCullough, and District Judge Valjean Biddison, and he would see what he could do. Even as the city was quickly devolving into chaos, proper procedures had to be followed to get the state troops into Tulsa.

The fires started at around 1:00 a.m. White people knew how valuable the homes, businesses, schools, churches, and other property were to the Black community, which had worked so hard to build up Greenwood over the years after being shut out of white neighborhoods in Oklahoma and many other states before settling there. So white people began setting fire to Black homes and businesses along Archer Street, torching building after building. Before the sun would come up, the mob would set fire to more than twenty-four Black businesses, including the Midway Hotel.

On the other side of the train tracks, the local National Guard was gathered at the armory on Sixth Street, where just hours before, the white mob had tried to steal weapons and ammunition. However, the Tulsa National Guard, though tasked with protecting all residents, was not impartial. Many members of the all-white unit also believed the trouble had started due to a "Negro uprising," and almost immediately, they began patrolling the Greenwood District, rounding up Black people and turning them over to the police, even as the Black community was clearly under attack.

Some Black Tulsans had fled town hours before, terrified of the violence that had already overtaken the city. Irene Scofield told the *Black Dispatch* newspaper: "Early in the evening when there was first talk of trouble, I and about forty others started out of the town and walked to a little town about fifteen miles away." Unfortunately, Billy Hudson, who had gathered his grandchildren and was setting out in their horse-drawn wagon for Nowata, a town about forty miles northeast of Tulsa, never made it. He, like many others, was killed by white people before their journey could begin.

Major Kirkpatrick had been working to get the signatures

for authorization to send the state troops, but the task was proving difficult among all the turmoil—especially when it came to Sheriff McCullough, who was still protecting Dick Rowland at the courthouse. But, finally, he obtained all the signatures, and at 1:46 a.m., sent the following telegram via Western Union:

```
Race riot developed here. Several killed.
  Unable handle situation.
Request that National Guard forces be sent
  by special train.
Situation serious.
```

When the gunfire at the railroad tracks stopped around 2:00 a.m., some people in the Black community, including *Tulsa Star* editor A. J. Smitherman, mistakenly assumed the fight was over, that they had prevailed. Unfortunately, many more hours of destruction and violence awaited them.

Rumors about the "Negro uprising" had spread to various white communities, including a story that a train full of five hundred armed Black people from Muskogee, Oklahoma, about fifty miles northwest of Tulsa, was headed into the Midland Valley Railway station off Third Street. At about 2:30 a.m., a group of white men with guns, plus a member of the National Guard, hurried over to the station, only to find that the train, of course, didn't exist. But the rumors persisted. One began to spread that a white woman had been killed by Black men shooting into white houses on Sunset Hill, north of Standpipe Hill. The National Guard believed this, too, and, taking a machine gun with them, deployed down Sunset Hill, which overlooked the Greenwood District. They eventually moved to Detroit Avenue between Brady Street and Standpipe Hill, establishing a "skirmish line" that directly faced the Black neighborhood.

Meanwhile, armed white people started organizing around the city to meet the supposed threat head-on. They began trading ammunition and agreed to head into Greenwood as soon as the sun came up.

"Men, we are going in at daylight," a white man declared to a group at Second and Lewis Streets that "Choc" Phillips, the white teenager who'd seen the Black man shot at the movie theater, estimated to be about six hundred in total.

"Be ready at daybreak," another white man instructed. "Nothing can stop us."

Approximately one hundred Oklahoma National Guard troops boarded a train to Tulsa at 5:00 a.m. on June 1, but several groups of armed white people—which some estimate were collectively as large as five to ten thousand people—were already planning their attacks. One group set up a machine gun on top of the Middle States Milling Company's grain elevator off of First Street so that it could fire straight into Greenwood.

And then, at 5:08 a.m., some sort of signal sounded. Maybe a siren, or perhaps a whistle; it's unknown where the sound emerged from and if it was an intentional signal for attack. Regardless, when the sound echoed throughout white Tulsa, hordes of white people with guns stormed across the railroad tracks and into Greenwood.

"With wild frenzied shouts, men began pouring from behind the freight depot and the long string of boxcars," an eyewitness recalled. "From every place of shelter up and down the tracks came screaming, shouting men to join in the rush toward the Negro section."

The men who had positioned the machine gun on top of the grain elevator began shooting north of Greenwood Avenue. The daybreak assault had officially begun—and Black Tulsans were terribly outnumbered. They had to make the difficult decision of whether to protect the homes and property they had worked so hard to build, or save the lives of themselves and their families and flee Tulsa.

Mary Elizabeth Jones Parrish, who was with her daughter, Florence Mary, in her apartment at 105 North Greenwood Avenue, was one of those people. She finally decided to leave, later writing, "I did not take time to get a hat for myself or [my daughter], but started out north on Greenwood, running amidst showers of bullets from the machine gun located in the granary and from men who were quickly surrounding our district. . . . Someone called to me to 'Get out of the street with that child or you both will be killed.' I felt it was suicide to remain in the building, for it would surely be destroyed and death in the street was preferred, for we expected to be shot down at any moment." Mary and Florence Mary eventually made it to the home of a friend who lived over Standpipe Hill.

Alice Andrews somehow managed to sleep through the early-morning chaos, "but my mother witnessed the riot and the aftermath. She said she sat at her living room window all night watching those people running down the [railroad] tracks, just running and running and trying to get away from the horrors of the riot. There were no paved roads in North Tulsa then. That is why the women and children were running down the railroad tracks, so they could keep out of the mud. The women were still in their nightgowns and they were holding their children's hands and just dragging them along. The children were crying."

Soon, the armed white Tulsans on the ground weren't the only threat—the Greenwood District was being attacked from the sky. Planes, piloted by white men, were circling the neighborhood and flying low to the ground. City officials, pushing back against the idea that they had any involvement, would later maintain that the two-seater, single-engine aircraft were used to monitor what was happening below. But several survivors and witnesses remember the planes dropping explosives, adding to the fires that were being set throughout the district. There is evidence in at least one case of men tossing what was thought to be dynamite sticks from a plane, and it is likely there were also men in the planes firing rifles and pistols. The district's first Black physician, the esteemed Dr. R. T. Bridgewater, remembered: "Aeroplanes began to fly over us, in some instances very low to the ground. A cry was heard from the women saying, 'Look out for the aeroplanes, they are shooting upon us.'"

Attorney B. C. Franklin witnessed the planes, as well; he wrote, "From my office window, I could see planes circling in midair. They grew in number and hummed, darted and dipped low. I could hear something like hail falling upon the top of my office building. Down East Archer, I saw the old Mid-Way Hotel on fire, burning from its top, and then another and another and another building began to burn from the top. . . . Lurid flames roared and belched and licked their forked tongues in the air. Smoke ascended the sky in thick, black volumes and amid it all, the planes—now a dozen or more in number—still hummed and darted here and there with the agility of natural birds of the air."

Meanwhile, the white mob that had stocked up on ammunition and guns, and had been deputized by the Tulsa police, had invaded Greenwood. They yanked people from their homes, forcing them out at gunpoint. They stole guns or rifles they found on Black men, then led the men away to holding areas, often separating them from their wives and children, who were forced to flee to their safety alone. Then white looters—including women, who were seen carrying shopping bags—stormed into the Black-owned businesses and homes, stealing whatever they found to be of value and destroying what they knew would personally hurt the families and business owners. Finally, they set fire to the houses and buildings; the arsonists' weapons of choice were torches and rags soaked in oil.

Men in khaki uniforms, likely veterans from World War I, were responsible for setting some of these fires. And Tulsa police officers were observed to be partaking in the violence as well, alongside the appointed "special deputies."

Black Tulsan Carrie Kinlaw was thrown into the line of fire as she tried to rescue her sick mother. "My sisters and I gathered her up, placed her on a cot, and three of us carried the cot and the other one carried a bundle of clothes," she remembered.

"Thus we carried Mother about six blocks, with bullets falling on all sides. About six squads of rioters overtook us, asked for men and guns, made us hold up our hands." She noted that "there were boys in that bunch, from about ten years upward, all armed with guns."

White Tulsan Harold M. Parker recalled the "sheer cruelty" of the white rioters, some of whom fired bullets at the feet of the Black people they took prisoner, marching them to Convention Hall on West Brady Street to be rounded up. "Sometimes they missed and shot their legs," Parker said.

A man is detained by the white mob on June 1, 1921, standing on the south side of the Frisco railroad tracks near North Cincinnati Avenue. The Oklahoma Pipe & Supply Company at 2 N. Cincinnati is pictured behind him, to the right.

A postcard depicting Black men being marched to Convention Hall on June 1, 1921

Cruelty certainly played a part in the death of famed Greenwood physician Dr. A. C. Jackson. White retired judge and former city commissioner John Oliphant recalled seeing his forty-two-year-old neighbor in the last few moments of his life. Jackson, who had worked until late in the night at Booker T. Washington Hospital helping those wounded from the massacre, returned to his home at 523 North Detroit around three in the morning. He'd sent his wife away once rumors of the mob violence had started.

Later that morning, Oliphant saw Dr. Jackson outside his house, standing in front of a group of armed white men in khaki uniforms. Dr. Jackson knew they'd been taking Black people to Convention Hall, and he had his hands in the air, ready to surrender.

"Here I am," Dr. Jackson said. "I want to go with you."

Oliphant tried to come to his defense. He told the white men who the doctor was, saying, "Don't hurt him." Oliphant pleaded with them to spare Dr. Jackson's life. But one of the men "shot him twice and the other fellow on the other side . . . shot him and broke his leg."

Dr. Jackson was taken to Convention Hall, where he later died from his injuries.

Armed white civilians, the Tulsa police force, and the local National Guard were all working in tandem to disempower the Black Americans fighting for their lives. They ignored the armed white people who were injuring and killing innocent Black children and adults. They ignored the blind, disabled Black man being dragged behind a car down Main Street with a rope around what remained of his amputated leg. They ignored the arsonists setting fire to Black businesses and homes, and instead worked to round up the Black community, taking them to internment camps where they were imprisoned solely because they were Black (though officials later claimed this was for their own safety). Firefighters were threatened by armed white people when they attempted to put out the fires in Greenwood, despite the fact that the plumes of black smoke rising in the sky over the African American neighborhood could be seen from miles away.

Though many Black Tulsans left town for their safety, Black veteran Seymour Williams was far from the only one who stayed to fight for Greenwood. Scores of residents put their lives at risk to defend their community.

B. C. Franklin came across the intersection of North Greenwood and East Easton and saw the home of a young Black World War I veteran, John Ross, was on fire. He had run into Ross earlier that day, who had returned to Tulsa from out of state, after "something within me told me that all was not well at home." Ross had informed him, "I'm going back home to defend it or die in the attempt."

Franklin wrote, "On the front porch stood Mother Ross, with outstretched and trembling hands, begging a mob that was approaching from the northwest to spare her home and family. . . . From within I could hear the report of high-powered rifles. I remembered the words of young Ross and knew he was making good on his threat. Every time there was a report of a gun from within, one of the members of the mob would fall, never to rise again. I somehow, felt happy. I cannot explain that feeling. I never felt that way—before nor since."

Over on Elgin Avenue, a group of Black men climbed up to the belfry of the newly constructed Mount Zion Baptist Church, which had held its first services in the new building only a couple of months before. In the end, their efforts to save the church were futile. The white rioters had set up a machine gun across the way, and the bullets tore through the building, which was set on fire not long afterward. But the Greenwood residents had fought to save it, for as long as they could.

Mount Zion Baptist Church at 421 N. Elgin Avenue, set on fire by the white mob. The new building had been completed only two months prior to the massacre.

One of the greatest legends of the Tulsa Race Massacre is that of Horace "Peg Leg" Taylor, a Black World War I veteran. By one account, Taylor was single-handedly responsible for killing dozens of white rioters while stationed at Standpipe Hill for more than six hours. According to another, he was part of a group of men who gathered behind Paradise Baptist Church, formed a human chain, and headed out with guns to protect Greenwood. Still, others claim that he died during the massacre, although there is evidence from census records and a draft card from World War II that show he was still living in Tulsa in the 1930s and 1940s.

Though it's unclear if there was any truth in the varying stories, Taylor's fierce determination to defend his neighborhood no doubt made an impact on the survivors of the massacre. He eventually moved to Arizona, where he remarried a minister. According to his death certificate from 1973, he died in Phoenix as a minister himself.

The white rioters were large in numbers, but some white people did try to help Black Tulsans that day. Several Black people lived with their white employers, who knew what was happening and didn't want them to be harmed. LaVerne Cooksey Davis, who worked as a live-in housekeeper for a white doctor, remembered those early-morning hours clearly: "I had gone to bed and after midnight, I got a telephone call from the doctor who was still downtown. . . . He told me not to go into Little Africa. . . . I thought that was strange for him to tell me that. I wouldn't have been going into North Tulsa at that late hour anyway," she said. "Well, later on the doctor called me again, and this time he was more urgent in telling me not to go into Little Africa. He said, 'Hell has broken out in Little Africa. Don't go down there!'"

Some of the Black people who worked in white homes still lived in Greenwood, and so they fled to the south side of the railroad tracks when the violence began to seek out safety in those homes. While plenty of domestic workers were rounded up at gunpoint by the white rioters and taken downtown, others were protected by their white employers, who hid them or straight up refused to let the rioters kidnap them.

White Tulsan Mary Jo Erhardt hid a Black porter named Jack who worked at the YWCA Building on Fifth Street and Cheyenne Avenue, where she lived. She pushed him into the walk-in refrigerator and remembered, "Hardly had I hidden him behind the beef carcasses and returned to the hall door when a loud pounding at the service entrance drew me there." Three "very rough-looking middle-aged white men" were standing on the stoop, trying to get at the porter.

"I was so angry I could have torn those ruffians apart," she said. "Three armed white men chasing one lone, harmless Negro. I cannot recall in all my life feeling hatred toward any person, until then." Erhardt told them, "I'm not letting *anybody* in here!" And she didn't, ultimately saving Jack's life.

Maria Morales Gutierrez, a Mexican immigrant, is another hero from that day, saving two young Black children from airplanes swooping down on them in the street. She was later confronted by armed white men, who told her to give up the small children, but she said no, and as her daughter Gloria Lough later remembered, "Somehow or other, they didn't shoot her." Because of Gutierrez, the children were not harmed.

And a Jewish family, the Zarrows, who owned a grocery store at 1427 East Sixth Street, also acted selflessly that day. Henry Zarrow, who was a child at the time, said, "I remember we hid people in our basement. My mother hid some of the little kids under her skirts."

The Oklahoma National Guard finally arrived in Tulsa by train, at about 9:15 a.m. But the damage was already done. The Greenwood District had been severely burned, white people were still looting the homes and businesses they hadn't yet torched, and dozens of people, both Black and white, were dead or injured. The Black survivors had either successfully made it outside of Tulsa to rural areas, or had been imprisoned at one of the internment centers at Convention Hall on Brady Street, the fairgrounds at Twenty-First Street and Yale Avenue, or McNulty Park's baseball field at Tenth Street and Elgin Avenue. People who thought it was safe to come out of hiding were quickly rounded up, as well.

The state troops finally declared martial law at 11:29 a.m. and began disarming white people and forcing them out of the Greenwood District. Like the local National Guard, the state troops were all white, but according to witness Mary Elizabeth Jones Parrish: "They used no partiality in quieting the disorder." However, she added, "It is the general belief that if they had reached the scene sooner, many lives and valuable property would have been saved." The state troops were joined by guardsmen from other parts of Oklahoma that day, and shortly thereafter they were able to clear all the white rioters from the streets. The troops instituted a curfew in Tulsa, mandating all businesses to close by 6:00 p.m., and ordering everyone except military, local authorities, relief workers, and physicians to stay in their homes after 7:00 p.m.

At 8:00 p.m. on June 1, the Tulsa Race Massacre was officially over.

In all this commotion, my grandmother didn't know where I was. I was missing from her for two days and she was so worried. She was just sick with grief. She thought I had been killed. A few days after the riot, blacks were released from detention and most were reunited with their families. But some people were not reunited. Some were never heard of again, like the [family] who took me to safety in their wagon pulled by the two mules. My grandparents tried and tried to locate them after the riot, and when I grew older, I tried to locate them, but they were never heard of again. I wonder if they were buried in some secret place.

—**Simon R. Richardson**,
Tulsa Race Massacre survivor

6

The Aftermath

What might have felt like a nightmare to Black survivors of the Tulsa Race Massacre was, unfortunately, a horrific reality. And once the smoke cleared, things didn't look any better.

Forced into internment centers after their homes and businesses were destroyed, Black Tulsans were refugees in their own town. The detainees had first been marched to Convention Hall on Brady Street, but after that building filled to capacity, the rioters began using other locations, including the fairgrounds and the minor league baseball stadium at McNulty Park. The National Guard also took part, delivering Black Tulsans who had made it to the countryside or who'd hidden out at Golden Gate Park to the internment camps.

James T. West, an educator at Booker T. Washington High

School, remembered that "people were herded in like cattle" to Convention Hall, saying, "The sick and wounded were dumped in front of the building and remained without attention for hours." The Black residents, who had been forced to walk to the internment centers—many of them at gunpoint, with their hands in the air like prisoners—were further humiliated and abused when some white rioters stole whatever items they'd managed to bring with them before their homes were burned to the ground.

Black Tulsans walking in downtown Tulsa on the morning of June 1, 1921

Some Black people were lucky enough to escape the camps altogether, heading to nearby towns such as Claremore and

Bartlesville. Others made their way to Missouri, where they were safe in Kansas City. And others left town without a trace, never to be heard from again.

The American Red Cross was called in for relief efforts, and after seeing all the wounded survivors and overall destruction in Greenwood, Red Cross representative Maurice Willows pleaded with headquarters to classify the incident as a natural disaster. Designating it as such allowed the Red Cross to act quickly, sending relief workers and building a temporary school and hospital in Tulsa. According to the organization's records, 183 Black people received surgery for their wounds immediately after the massacre, and 70 percent of those patients had to remain in the hospital for further care. Within the first week of the tragedy, doctors performed 163 additional surgeries, 82 of them considered "major" procedures. Eleven of the twenty doctors who worked on patients were Black. The National Guard armory on Sixth Street, where the white mob had tried to steal guns and ammunition before the riot began, was used as a clinic for wounded Black Tulsans, as the Black hospital had been burned to the ground. Some Black survivors in critical condition were even transferred to white hospitals, which was nearly unheard of in segregated Oklahoma.

Eventually, Willows and his team would help ensure the many Black Tulsans who'd been left homeless had temporary shelter, though for some people, that meant they were forced to stay at the fairgrounds camp, which was home to around five thousand people at one time, about half the Black population in Tulsa in 1921. The Red Cross raised $100,000 in funding to help the victims, and the NAACP and Universal Negro Improvement Association sent money for relief and legal efforts, too. The Colored Citizens Relief Committee, the East End Welfare Board, the Salvation Army, several churches, and some individuals also donated time and money to help the survivors of the massacre.

Still, while many Black Tulsans were freed from the internment centers within a matter of hours, others had to live there for weeks or several months, even during winter. It all depended on who they knew, and, crucially, if they were employed by white people. The rule was that if a white person came down to vouch for a Black person, they would be released and forced to wear a "green card" to show that their release had been approved. If they didn't possess or wear the card, they could be arrested.

Educator J. W. Hughes would later say, "Mr. Oberholtzer, city superintendent of public schools, came and called for all colored teachers, and we were taken to the old city high school,

IDENTIFICATION CARD

Name _____

Sex_____ Age_____

Where Living_____

Employed by_____

Address_____ Phone_____

Kind of Work_____

Employer's Signature _____

Card Approved_____

Date_____

The green ID card Black Tulsans were forced to carry after the massacre where I met my wife again. All the lady teachers were taken to the homes of the city principals and cared for nicely. We were allowed to stay in the old high school all night. . . . Miss Kimble of the domestic science department of the white high school gave us our breakfast."

Mary Elizabeth Jones Parrish said, "Every Negro was accorded the same treatment, regardless of his education or other advantages. A Negro was a Negro on that day." This was clear in not only the murder of such prominent figures as Dr. A. C. Jackson, but in how well-known and respected Black survivors fared afterward. Assistant county physician Dr. R. T. Bridgewater went to work helping victims and patients during the day, but he had to return to the camps at night since his Greenwood home had been destroyed in the fires. Black architect and contractor J. C. Latimer was also forced to stay at the camps. Though he was self-employed—a sign of success, especially in those days—that meant he didn't have a white person to vouch for him. He was released only after he persuaded a white man to pretend to know him, saying he was his brother-in-law so he could be set free.

Although they had shelter, the people in internment camps often came down with diseases. According to the Red Cross, there were at least eight cases of premature childbirth that ended in death, and of the pregnant women treated by Red Cross doctors, "practically all have presented complications due to the riot." Some people in the camps suffered from malnutrition, possibly because they had to pay for their own food; if they didn't have money, they had to work for their meals.

And in some cases, they were put to work cleaning up their very own neighborhood that had been destroyed by white rioters. They were also forced to confront the damage that had been done; per the Red Cross report, more than 1,250 homes had been burned, and 215 more that were spared torching had still been looted. The property damage of both the homes and businesses was estimated at just under $2 million, which totals nearly $30 million today. Still, some sources believe the damage was vastly underestimated and would currently account for anywhere from $50 million to $200 million. That damage included many businesses that had become the cornerstone of the Greenwood District. Mabel Little had lost her beauty shop. The *Tulsa Star* offices were gone. The brand-new Mount Zion Baptist Church building had been torched, as had the Black public library. H. L. Byars's tailor shop was gone, and so was Elliott & Hooker's Clothing Emporium. The white mob had even burned down the Williams family's Dreamland Theatre.

But for many, property loss was only part of their pain. The city issued thirty-seven death certificates for the massacre—twenty-five Black men and twelve white men, all dead from gunshot wounds or burning. Nine of the Black victims had been burned so badly they could not be identified, and a stillborn Black baby was found during the shooting and fires. But those statistics are thought to be extremely conservative; several historians' estimates average that as many as three hundred died, the majority of the victims Black. Many more were wounded.

ALL THAT WAS LEFT OF HIS HOME
AFTER TULSA RACE RIOT - 6-1-1921

A postcard depicting a Black man standing in the ruins of his home on June 1, 1921

One reason the death toll is so largely disputed is the fact that many survivor accounts recall witnessing the disposal of bodies of murder victims that were never counted. Black community activist Opal Long Dargan, who was five years old in 1921, remembered "some bodies had been unceremoniously dumped into the Arkansas River." Others, like white Tulsan Ross T. Warner, saw bodies carted away on trucks or flatbed railroad cars; Black Tulsan Henry C. Whitlow, who would go on to become principal of Booker T. Washington High School, claimed to have seen more than two dozen bodies driven away. And some people reported other Black victims were incinerated at Newblock Park, which was also home to Tulsa's landfill at the time.

Some city officials later claimed that "all those who were killed were given decent burials," but for years, Black and white Tulsans alike have maintained that the city has a substantial number of mass graves holding massacre victims. A mass grave is a grave containing two or more human corpses, typically buried without a proper funeral service, coffins, or tombstones. They have been used to bury bodies during wars, famines, natural disasters, and in the midst of epidemics and pandemics to control the spread of diseases. Mass graves were used for victims of the 1918 influenza pandemic, which killed about fifty million people worldwide. And the Nazi Party notoriously buried the bodies of millions of Jewish people in European mass graves during the Holocaust, twenty years after the Tulsa Race Massacre, in the 1940s.

Tulsans didn't have to wait long to find out who would be blamed for the massacre—and the news was likely unsurprising to the residents of Greenwood. A grand jury had been assembled, which was presided over by District Judge Valjean Biddison, and officiated by State Attorney General S. P. Freeling with assistance from Kathryn Van Leuven, Oklahoma's first female prosecuting attorney. In a June 25 report, the grand jury stated: "We find that the recent race riot was the direct result of an effort on the part of a certain group of colored men who appeared at the courthouse on the night of May 31, 1921. . . . There was no mob spirit among the whites, no talk of lynching and no arms. The assembly was quiet until the arrival of armed Negroes, which precipitated and was the direct cause of the entire affair."

In other words, the grand jury blamed the men trying to stop the promised violence instead of the ones who had gathered to lynch Dick Rowland, murdered with abandon when they didn't get their way, and left a destroyed community in their wake.

The grand jury also indicted nearly ninety people, primarily Black men, including Greenwood cofounder, businessman, and hotel owner J. B. Stradford. Stradford fled Tulsa after the indictment, only to be arrested in Independence, Kansas, two days later. Oklahoma newspaper the *Okmulgee Times* wasted no time in accusing him of inciting the violence, writing: "If Governor Allen of Kansas wants to help the authorities fix the blame for the rioting at Tulsa last week" he would "not refuse to" send Stradford back to Oklahoma. "Stradford, a generally undesirable citizen, can probably tell as much as anyone about the real cause of the trouble in Tulsa." J. B. Stradford's son, an attorney from Chicago, helped his father get his freedom from the Kansas authorities, and Stradford never returned to Tulsa. He settled down in Chicago, where he once again worked as a successful attorney and businessman.

Although white *Tulsa Tribune* editor Richard Lloyd Jones clearly helped instigate the race massacre with his incendiary article about Dick Rowland and his alleged editorial, *Tulsa Star* editor A. J. Smitherman would ultimately end up paying the price, both in his career and personal life. Not only was the Black journalist's entire newspaper office, printing press, and home destroyed in the massacre, but he was thrown in jail for charges related to rioting—organizing armed Black men to defend Dick Rowland and the residents of Greenwood—and indicted by a Tulsa grand jury. Smitherman eventually posted bail and fled Tulsa with his wife and kids. They started new lives halfway across the country, first in Massachusetts, then in Buffalo, New York, where Smitherman founded another newspaper. He ran the *Buffalo Star* (later renamed the *Empire Star*) from 1932 until his death in 1961; the paper folded soon thereafter. Smitherman never did face prosecution for the alleged crime of inciting a riot.

Not only were Black people blamed for the massacre, but they were also punished for crimes they didn't commit. Black Tulsans were barred from buying or even possessing guns for several weeks afterward. They were also not allowed to visit servants' quarters in white neighborhoods, except for "those employed regularly on the premises."

Conversely, no white people were ever imprisoned for the murders and property destruction over the eighteen hours they terrorized Greenwood. One person was held accountable for his actions that day, however: The negligent police chief John Gustafson, who abandoned the courthouse as the mob steadily assembled the evening of May 31, was found guilty of "dereliction of duty" and fired from his job. According to the *Tulsa World*, Judge Oliphant, the man who witnessed the murder of A. C. Jackson, testified that one of the men who'd confronted the doctor was a Tulsa police officer—who was either currently serving or had previously been on the force—named Brown, but that he couldn't identify who had shot his neighbor. None of the men were charged for Dr. Jackson's murder.

Although Black Tulsans had witnessed friends and family members being murdered or dragged away, never to be seen again, and lost their homes, businesses, and valuables, they were resilient. Many of them tried to rebuild soon after the dust settled, but their efforts were thwarted by the Tulsa City Commission, which passed a new fire code that stated all property in the Greenwood District must be rebuilt with fireproof materials. This amended code meant most Black Tulsans looking to rebuild couldn't afford the required materials and amounted to a clear attempt to prohibit the reconstruction of Greenwood. At the same time, a group of white businessmen tried to force Greenwood residents to rebuild farther to the northeast end of the city so that it could use the cleared district to build warehouses. They ultimately failed, as they couldn't raise money for their plan, and the Oklahoma Supreme Court later overturned the new fire code, declaring it illegal, which allowed Greenwood residents to rebuild in earnest.

And rebuild they did—though it would never be the same Greenwood. Several of the influential community members, like Stradford, Smitherman, and O. W. Gurley, who left Tulsa for Los Angeles, would never return. Others would settle down in towns outside of Tulsa, too traumatized by what had occurred to start all over in what had once been a city of promise. And the Black Tulsans who did want to stay and rebuild were being sabotaged at every turn; insurance companies denied the majority of the property claims because the massacre was categorized as a "riot," a circumstance that was automatically excluded from

The Williams Dreamland Theatre, located at 129 N. Greenwood Avenue, after being destroyed by the white mob

most insurance policies. The only business owner to receive compensation for their losses was a white pawnshop owner, who was reimbursed for the nearly $4,000 in guns and ammunition that were stolen by the white mob.

Another white property owner filed a lawsuit against the Tulsa police force for its part in the massacre, but despite the witnesses he provided who recounted they'd seen police officers destroying the Greenwood District, the lawsuit was dismissed. Some people also claimed that the massacre had been planned by city authorities and the white community long before May 30, and that the incident between Dick Rowland and Sarah Page was just an excuse—or was even staged—for white people to destroy the Greenwood District. This has not been confirmed, though there is no denying tensions were running high between the white and Black communities well before Dick Rowland set foot in that elevator.

Speaking of Rowland—what happened to him and Page, whose interaction fueled the flames?

Page disappeared on June 1, and no one has been able to trace her whereabouts since 1921. And though it was the arrest of Dick Rowland that started it all, by June 1 he was all but forgotten as Greenwood was looted and burned. According to the *Tulsa World*, the prosecuting attorneys dismissed all charges against Rowland, "purportedly at the written request of Page." After spending the night in the courthouse jail, Rowland also left town, never to be seen again. Rumors abounded, including that Page and Rowland were in fact romantically linked and had met up in Kansas City before parting ways. However, there is no proof that happened, nor is there any documentation that Rowland died in the Pacific Northwest, one common line of speculation.

The Tulsa Race Massacre seemed to be over as quickly as it had begun, with Black Tulsans left to fend for themselves as they attempted to rebuild after such tragedy. With the judicial system and public officials unwilling to take responsibility for the violence, murder, and destruction of property that had ravaged Black Wall Street, the residents of Greenwood had no choice but to look forward for hope and healing. But as they planned for their future, white Tulsans and Oklahomans alike wouldn't give them the dignity of openly mourning all that had been lost. Many white people who had lived through the Tulsa Race Massacre wanted nothing more than to bury the past.

Until Tulsa does right by Greenwood,
this district will forever be a crime scene.

—Reverend Dr. Robert Turner,
Vernon African Methodist Episcopal Church,
Tulsa, Oklahoma

7

The Legacy of Greenwood

While many Tulsans at the time would have preferred that the whole incident be immediately forgotten, it wasn't—at least not at first. Dozens of newspapers around the country reported on the massacre: The *New York Times* ran a front-page story, and the appalling event even made international news, with a headline in the *Times of London*. In the United States, citizens from as far as Philadelphia and as near as Kansas were condemning Tulsa for what had taken place, calling the massacre a "horror" and a "disgrace."

Oklahomans were split on the national reaction to the event. Some white Tulsans seemed proud of what had happened. They bragged about their involvement and passed around postcards that displayed graphic photos of massacre victims, similar to the postcards and photographs that were distributed around the United States after lynchings of Black Americans. More than seventeen hundred members of the revamped Ku Klux Klan continued to terrorize Black Tulsans over the course of the following year. In April 1922, they paraded through downtown Tulsa—under an airplane that was flying an electrically lit cross. While it was never determined if the KKK was officially involved in the massacre, a number of Klan members were elected to Tulsa city and county office in 1922.

Some Black Tulsans did not want the event to be forgotten, for very different reasons. Mary Elizabeth Jones Parrish, a Black educator and journalist who survived the massacre with her daughter, Florence Mary, wrote about the massacre for the Oklahoma Interracial Commission, a group focused on preventing lynchings. Parrish recorded the event from her own memories, and transcribed interviews with witnesses, as well as testimonies of other survivors. Along with photographs detailing the damage that had been done, Parrish published her account in her 1922 book, *Events of the Tulsa Disaster*—the first to be published about the massacre.

However, it would be a long time before anything else recounting the event would be

Mary Elizabeth Jones Parrish

printed. Many people, including most public officials, didn't appreciate the widespread national criticism of their state. Oklahoma had been a state for only fourteen years at that time. It was still trying to establish itself in the United States, and a shameful event like the Greenwood massacre would only make people think that Tulsa was an unruly, violent, racist place to live. Political leaders and business owners didn't want the story of the massacre hanging over them.

Thus began a concerted effort to erase it from Oklahoma's history.

A prime example can be found in the archives of the *Tulsa Tribune*. While the paper had been so eager to report on Dick Rowland's alleged "assault," the subject of the ensuing massacre was conspicuously absent from future issues commemorating past events. In the 1930s, the paper published an editorial series called "Fifteen Years Ago" that shone a spotlight on events in Tulsa's past from the same day. The June 1936 issue, however, mentioned nothing about the massacre; instead, it highlighted parties from June 1921, news about people who had graduated from Tulsa high schools that year, and the goings-on of Tulsa residents, such as who was entertaining out-of-town visitors and who had gone on trips themselves. While one could assume that the *Tribune* believed it was too soon to rehash the massacre, ten years later, in June 1946, the newspaper once again ignored the subject in its "Twenty-Five Years Ago" feature.

Unfortunately, the *Tribune* wasn't the only publication or entity that tried to bury the truth. The Oklahoma volume of the *American Guide Series* mentioned it in 1941 but devoted only one paragraph to the subject. History textbooks completely ignored the event—in fact, it was not included as part of the state's public school curricula until 2000, nearly eighty years after the massacre. This resulted in near total erasure of what had happened in Greenwood, to the point that many people who moved to Tulsa after the massacre and even some born and raised there in the ensuing years, both Black and white, often knew nothing about it.

Educator Nancy Feldman, who was white, hadn't heard anything about the Tulsa Race Riot, as it was known then, when she moved to Oklahoma in 1946 to teach sociology at the University of Tulsa. Survivor Robert Fairchild informed her of the event that had occurred twenty-five years prior, and, deeply disturbed by what she'd learned, she brought up the incident with her college students. According to Feldman, several of them "stoutly denied it and questioned my facts." Even after Fairchild himself visited the all-white class, they were not convinced; even worse, their parents told them Fairchild and Feldman were lying. Feldman was ordered by the school's dean to "drop the whole subject." She said her own friends were reluctant to acknowledge what had happened, as well: "When I would mention the riot to my white friends, few would talk about it. And they certainly didn't want to."

Nancy Dodson, an instructor at Tulsa Junior College, was also advised not to talk about the massacre "almost upon our arrival," she said. "Because of shame, I thought. But the explanation was, 'You don't want to start another.'"

Of course, some white people *were* ashamed of what had

happened, while Black survivors were silent from fear, and likely not eager to speak of such a sad moment in their history. Perhaps some of them—close descendants of enslaved people, and some maybe even formerly enslaved themselves—didn't want to burden their children with such a harrowing tale about what had happened in their own town, and not that long ago.

It's not that the massacre wasn't discussed at all; it was, privately. But it had been made clear that public discussion was taboo, and most of the city's white residents, in particular, adhered to this collective oath of silence. Educational institutions in particular didn't seem to want their faculty to speak out about the massacre, even as trying to hide what had occurred was denying their students the Tulsa history and education they were paying for, and deserved.

Still, while University of Tulsa leaders may not have wanted instructors like Nancy Feldman to speak about the massacre, that didn't stop one of their students from writing his graduate thesis on the topic in 1946. Loren L. Gill, a white veteran of World War II, was fascinated by the massacre and began conducting extensive research and interviews with locals, city officials, and survivors. Although his paper is considered by historians to be somewhat reductive and inaccurate in its conclusions, Gill's efforts to record the truth of what happened in 1921 have been commended.

Despite the primarily white teachers and institutions who sought to hide what had happened, there are Black educators who tried their best to pass down the story of Black Wall Street and its demise. Some teachers at Booker T. Washington High School ensured their students knew the history of Greenwood in the years following.

But other than these few instances, the massacre largely remained lost to history.

Eventually, however, things started to change.

A few months before the fiftieth anniversary of the massacre, the head of the Tulsa chamber of commerce magazine decided to cover the event. Ed Wheeler, a white man who hosted a history show on a local radio station, was hired to write the article and began interviewing survivors and digging through local records. Not long after he started his research, other white people began trying to intimidate him; he received menacing phone calls, and groups of men twice approached him in person, plainly saying, "Don't write that story." Wheeler didn't give in to their threats, however, and finished the article—only for upper management at the chamber of commerce to block its publication, a decision that was backed up by the chamber's board of directors.

Like graduate student Gill, Wheeler was determined to report the truth about what had happened in 1921, and after the story was also rejected by Tulsa's two major newspapers, he ended up finding a home for it in a new Black publication called *Impact Magazine*.

There were also photographs taken of the massacre, many of which were preserved and housed in a collection at the Tulsa

Historical Society. For this, we must thank Mozella Franklin Jones, daughter of B. C. Franklin, the well-known Black attorney in Tulsa who had survived the massacre and represented other survivors and whose work also helped overturn the building codes that were implemented to prevent residents from rebuilding Greenwood.

Buck Colbert "B.C." Franklin

Also in 1971, Black survivors came together to remember the event with a special program at Mount Zion Baptist Church, whose original building had been torched during the massacre only a few weeks after it was dedicated. The fiftieth anniversary program was headed by W. D. Williams, known as Bill when he was a teenager—the son of John and Loula, who had owned several businesses in Greenwood, including the iconic Dreamland Theatre. The Williams family had survived, but their businesses, including the auto shop and confectionery, were destroyed in the massacre. Williams was one of the teachers at Booker T. Washington High School, his alma mater, who had worked to keep the massacre's memory alive. Some white people also attended the program at Mount Zion. It was the first time Tulsans had publicly recognized the massacre in decades.

The 1970s were a time of change. It was the first decade

after the passage of the landmark Civil Rights Act of 1964 and the Fair Housing Act of 1968, which promised Black people all over the country equal treatment by law. Black culture began to gain popularity around the United States, in the form of literature, television, and, significantly, in education, as the first programs and departments focused on Black studies had recently been established at select institutions (though many of these programs were often underfunded). And as education transformed, people began to talk and teach more about what had happened in Tulsa fifty years ago. Books about Oklahoma began to include accounts of it, too. In 1975, historian Rudia M. Halliburton Jr. published *The Tulsa Race War of 1921*, the first book about the massacre since Mary Elizabeth Jones Parrish's 1922 account.

As remarkable—and long overdue—as these efforts were, they did not overcome the forces of white supremacy that kept the stories of Greenwood hidden, nor did they bring them to light on a national scale. But they gave Tulsans and future historians a way to piece things together, little by little, even decades later.

While everyone was trying to decide how and when to talk about the massacre, what happened to Greenwood itself?

Only a few buildings in the thirty-plus blocks that were destroyed survived the massacre, including Booker T. Washington High School and Vernon African Methodist Episcopal Church. The high school desegregated in 1973 and began busing in white students to learn alongside local Black students. Now known as a magnet school, Booker T. Washington has changed locations twice since 1921, but the facade of the original building was transported and used in construction of the current building on East Zion Street "for its historical significance." Vernon A.M.E. Church, whose basement remained intact after the massacre, was later added to the National Register for Historic Places in 2018.

The *Oklahoma Eagle* Opens Up Shop

In June 1920, Black journalist Theodore Baughman, the managing editor of A. J. Smitherman's *Tulsa Star*, left his job and founded a competing newspaper, the *Oklahoma Sun*. However, just a year later, the Tulsa Race Massacre destroyed businesses in the Greenwood District, including the offices of both the *Sun* and the *Star*. Smitherman sold what could be salvaged of his equipment to Baughman and left town, making Baughman's publication the only Black newspaper in the city. Baughman reportedly put out a trimmed-down daily paper after the massacre, printing the names of people looking for family and friends.

Baughman changed the name of his paper to the *Oklahoma Eagle* and would eventually open an office in the rebuilt Greenwood District. In 1936, Edward L. Goodwin Sr. invested in the *Eagle*, and became sole owner the next year, after Baughman's death. Goodwin, who said he was going to dedicate the rest of his life to "fighting for the things that I knew that black people needed and never had in order to elevate them to a higher social level, a higher economic level, [than] they'd been accustomed to," created a new motto for the *Eagle*: "We Make America Better When We Aid Our People."

The *Oklahoma Eagle* is the tenth-oldest Black-owned newspaper currently publishing in the United States, and is the last original Black-owned business from Black Wall Street still operating in the Greenwood District footprint.

All that's currently left of the original Negro Wall Street is fourteen brick buildings at Greenwood Avenue and Archer Street, which were reconstructed after the massacre. But those buildings aren't the only reminders to mark the area where the neighborhood once stood. Dozens of street plaques commemorating the people and businesses of the Greenwood District, the first of which was installed in the early 1990s, line Greenwood Avenue, due to the efforts of Black Tulsa native Michael Reed.

"We developed our own community and that's something I'm really proud of and I want the world to know it," he told Tulsa's News on 6 in 2020. "It was a shame to lose the recognition of the pioneers, the historic value and contribution of the citizens that were here in the early 1900s."

After working with local leaders in the 1990s to lay the first plaques, installation continued in the mid-2000s, with the assistance of Reuben Gant, who was then serving as president of the Greenwood Chamber of Commerce. "It was a way to pay homage to the story of Greenwood," Gant said. "It created a sense of identity and I notice people walking through the district with their heads down and what they [are] doing is reading the plaques."

Today, more than 170 plaques detail the businesses that stood there before the massacre—their names, their street addresses, and whether they reopened. In 2019, people began reporting they were damaged, missing, or in such poor shape that the text could no longer be read. Construction crews working in the area maintained they would reinstall any plaques that were dug up while working, and Reed said there are plans to install more in the future.

By the 2010s, Greenwood had become a racially mixed neighborhood with a growing business district. It contains a minor league baseball stadium for hometown team the Tulsa Drillers, an arts district, a luxury apartment complex, a shopping center, and more. But not everyone is happy about these changes: In 2018, the *Washington Post* reported that some of the African American residents of Greenwood, who make up two-thirds of the neighborhood, had mixed feelings about increasing development for white-owned businesses in a neighborhood where non-Black people may not even know the history.

However, some of the new construction has been regarded as a positive addition to the community. In 1995, the city spent $3 million on the Greenwood Cultural Center, a nonprofit organization at 322 North Greenwood Avenue that houses an event venue, a photo gallery, and space to host youth and community programs and classes. The complex also runs the Mabel B. Little Heritage House, which serves as a museum that honors

Little, a survivor, as well as victims of the massacre. In 2019, it was announced the Greenwood Cultural Center will undergo a $9 million expansion, funded by private donors, which will reconfigure the current structure and add administrative offices, a museum, and a gift shop.

The John Hope Franklin Center for Reconciliation was founded in 2007 and helped oversee construction of the John Hope Franklin Reconciliation Park, which opened in October 2010 on North Elgin Avenue. John Hope Franklin, the son of prominent Black lawyer and massacre survivor B. C. Franklin, was a highly respected educator, historian, and civil rights advocate; he died in 2009 but witnessed the groundbreaking of his eponymous park. It now includes an area called Hope Plaza, which displays three bronze sculptures based on people in photographs of the massacre, as well as the twenty-five-foot-tall Tower of Reconciliation, which depicts the history of Black Americans in Oklahoma, with a focus on the massacre. The park also hosts tours that include information on the massacre, the Trail of Tears, the migration of Black Americans, the Greenwood District, and Black Wall Street.

Despite the efforts made by these citizens and institutions to bring attention to Tulsa's history, as well as unity to a community so brutally fractured, many Black Tulsans don't feel the massacre has been given proper resolution. In 1997, an eleven-member state commission was formed to investigate the causes and consequences of the massacre and to give suggestions on how the city should address it moving forward. The Oklahoma

Commission to Study the Tulsa Race Riot of 1921 released a 178-page report in February 2001 that strongly recommended a series of reparations initiatives, including direct payment of reparations to survivors and descendants of the massacre, the creation of a scholarship fund for students affected by the massacre, the establishment of an economic development enterprise zone in the historic Greenwood District, and more.

Though Reconciliation Park was a result of the commission's study, the city has not implemented most of the commission's other recommendations. In 2003, a group of survivors and descendants attempted to sue the city, as well as the state of Oklahoma, for damages suffered from the massacre. The federal district court dismissed the case, claiming the victims had waited too long to file the lawsuit—in spite of the fact that public officials worked to cover up the case for decades, and information definitively stating police officers and other officials were directly involved in the massacre wasn't available until the commission delivered its report in 2001.

Nevertheless, the Tenth Circuit Court of Appeals agreed: "In fact, plaintiffs neither allege nor even imply that they were prohibited from accessing the courts in the 1970s, 1980s, or 1990s." The court believed the survivors and descendants should have done so after the civil rights laws passed in the 1960s, or after Scott Ellsworth's extensively researched book *Death in a Promised Land* was published in 1982. The group attempted to appeal the case once again two years later, in 2005, but the US Supreme Court declined to hear it, without comment. Black Tulsans have also unsuccessfully worked to get the district listed on the

National Register of Historic Places. Designating Black Wall Street as a national historic site would protect the commercial district from unwanted construction and allow Black Tulsans to make decisions on its legacy. Though two churches from the original district have been designated—Mount Zion Baptist and Vernon A.M.E.—the Oklahoma Historical Society and preservation officials believe it would be a challenge to get it listed, as almost all the buildings "of historic significance" that remained, including many that were rebuilt in the years following the massacre, were demolished by urban renewal efforts in the 1950s.

The Black Wall Street Massacre Memorial, located in Tulsa's Greenwood District, which honors the hundreds of Black Tulsans killed in 1921

While assessing how to best distribute reparations, the Tulsa Race Riot Commission brought to light a significant matter that has plagued survivors for decades: it recommended the creation of a memorial "for the reburial of any human remains found in the search for unmarked graves of riot victims."

In 1998, spurred by renewed attention to eyewitness survivor accounts that the bodies of Black victims had been dumped into mass graves around the city, investigators began probing for the remains in a number of likely areas. The digs found conditions "that merited further investigation." Then, in 1999, a white man named Clyde Eddy came forward with additional information. Ten years old at the time of the massacre, Eddy stated he saw white men digging a trench in a section of Tulsa's Oaklawn Cemetery in 1921. He also claimed to have seen wooden crates there, holding Black bodies. A follow-up of Eddy's claims led by world-renowned forensic anthropologist Clyde Snow revealed an "anomaly" that showed "all the characteristics of a dug pit or trench with vertical walls and an undefined object within the approximate center of the feature," per the commission report. The commission went on to say, "It can be argued that the geophysical study, combined with the account of Mr. Eddy, are compelling arguments for this feature being considered a mass grave." However, despite overwhelming evidence to support further investigation, the city declined to excavate this area of Oaklawn Cemetery. Susan Savage, Tulsa's mayor at the time, claimed she didn't want to disturb the marked graves at the site.

However, in 2018, Tulsa mayor G. T. Bynum committed to

launching another investigation. He told the *Washington Post*: "We owe it to the community to know if there are mass graves in our city. We owe it to the victims and their family members. We will do everything we can to find out what happened in 1921." And in July 2020, Tulsa finally began to dig for mass graves from the Tulsa Race Massacre at Oaklawn. Under observance from descendants of massacre survivors, archaeologists and forensic anthropologists began carefully digging, using machinery and techniques that would minimize damage to any remains they might find. The land was also excavated by hand. Unfortunately, the test excavations, though initially promising, did not yield anticipated results.

In October 2020, however, a forensics team "unearthed eleven coffins" while searching in another area of the cemetery, according to the *New York Times*. As the paper reported, "The mass grave was discovered in an area of the city's Oaklawn Cemetery where records and research suggested that as many as 18 victims would be found. Painstaking work will be required to identify whether the remains are from victims of the massacre."

The city has plans to continue digging in other areas of Oaklawn, as well as at the former Booker T. Washington Cemetery and around Newblock Park, two other areas where mass graves were presumed to have been dug.

The progress toward resolution has been slow, to say the least, but survivors—of which there are few, a hundred years after the massacre—and their descendants are still looking to move forward.

Hotel owner and Greenwood District cofounder J. B. Stradford had been indicted for charges related to the massacre; his charges were dropped in 1996 after his descendants petitioned the court to reexamine the case. Oklahoma governor Frank Keating also named October 18 of that year "J. B. Stradford Day," and Stradford, who successfully practiced law in Chicago after the massacre, was posthumously admitted to the Oklahoma Bar Association.

The city of Tulsa sought to make further amends in 2007 when Tulsa County district attorney Tim Harris dismissed all the indictments that were issued to Greenwood residents in 1921—including the indictment of *Tulsa Star* newspaper publisher A. J. Smitherman.

The Tulsa Race Massacre in Pop Culture (Spoilers Ahead!)

Many people had never heard of the Tulsa Race Massacre until the premiere of HBO's limited series *Watchmen* in October 2019. Graphically depicting the massacre in the beginning of the first episode, the series uses the event as part of the origin story of the world's first superhero. Viewers later learn that the main character's grandfather was one of the survivors fighting for his life in the distressing flashback.

Though the series constructs an alternate history—in the 2019 Tulsa of *Watchmen*, survivors and their descendants have already been granted reparations under the leadership of

Robert Redford, who'd been the US president for decades—the show displays a deep respect for Greenwood's history, incorporating homages to the Dreamland Theatre and the Greenwood Cultural Center, as well as iconic photographs of the massacre. *Watchmen* was nominated for twenty-six Emmys and won eleven, both of which were the most of any show at the 2020 ceremony. When series creator Damon Lindelof accepted the Emmy for outstanding limited series, he dedicated the statue to massacre victims and survivors.

Another HBO series, *Lovecraft Country*, delves into the Tulsa Race Massacre; the main character, Atticus, is the descendant of massacre survivors, and a poignant flashback episode depicts scenes with younger versions of his father and uncle on the evening of May 31, 1921.

For decades, the Tulsa Race Massacre was considered a taboo subject, but in recent years, people have been talking about it more than ever. Many books, both nonfiction and historical novels, have been written on the subject, documentaries have been produced, and television and podcast series have dedicated extensive air time to the massacre. The Smithsonian's National Museum of African American History and Culture in Washington, DC, houses a manuscript from survivor B. C. Franklin; he wrote a detailed firsthand account of the massacre, which was found in 2015 and donated to the museum "with the support of the Franklin family." The museum also created a section called "Riot and Resilience in Tulsa, Oklahoma" in its Power of Place exhibition.

The 1921 Tulsa Race Massacre Centennial Commission was formed by Oklahoma State senator Kevin Matthews in 2017 to "leverage the history surrounding the events of nearly 100 years ago by developing programs, projects, events and activities to commemorate and inform." The organization is building a history center in Greenwood, helped the Oklahoma State Department of Education develop curriculum to teach the massacre to public school students around the state, is offering a three-day workshop to Oklahoma social studies teachers to aid in teaching about the massacre, and has received a $1 million grant to fund the Greenwood Art Project.

In 2018, the Black Wall Street Chamber of Commerce was created "to enhance the quality of life for African Americans and the north Tulsa community through economic development, education, workforce development, community development, and legislative advocacy." The chamber is hoping to rebuild the Greenwood commercial district, as well as the surrounding area in North Tulsa.

And in September 2020, ninety-nine years after the massacre, another group of survivors and descendants filed a new lawsuit against the city of Tulsa, as well as six other defendants that includes the Oklahoma National Guard, the Tulsa County sheriff, and the Tulsa Regional Chamber, the city's chamber of commerce. The lawsuit seeks to gain unspecified punitive damages, but also focuses on reparations in the form of scholarships, as well as awarding city contracts to Black-owned businesses. The attorneys representing the survivors and victims are hoping the court will rule that the massacre was a "public nuisance," which is "unlawfully doing an act" that "endangers the comfort, repose, health, or safety of others"—an overdue designation that the erasure of history has long prevented.

Tulsan Eddie Faye Gates donated a large collection of "eyewitness accounts, photographs, recorded survivor stories and other narratives of the 1921 Tulsa Race Massacre" to Tulsa's Gilcrease Museum in late 2020. The Gilcrease has used the nearly $300,000 in grant money it received from the Institute of Museum and Library Services to digitize the collection, which includes newspaper clippings, audio and video interviews with survivors, and Gates's handwritten research notes, among other items.

"It became her mission to ensure the atrocities that occurred during the 1921 Race Massacre are not forgotten and that the survivors' stories serve to make needed change," Dianne Gates-Anderson, Gates's daughter, told the *Tulsa World*. "It is also important to her and our family that the collection be physically located in North Tulsa and accessible for viewing and research by descendants and the community at large." The museum works with the provided materials to "create resources for teaching such trauma-based history topics for K–12 educators." At long last, educators and students will have a wealth of significant and personal information about a story that has long been whispered about or simply hidden.

Perhaps nobody could say it better than Tulsa Race Massacre

survivor descendant John Hope Franklin, when he spoke at the dedication to the park named in his honor in 2008: "Someday we'll have the joy and pleasure of complete reconciliation. We're moving in that direction. I hope we get there very soon."

One has to wonder why such a remarkable feat as Black Wall Street and the tragic story of the Tulsa Race Massacre went untold for so long—and why this is just one event in a long line of American triumphs and tragedies that have been erased from history books for decades or even centuries. In essence, white supremacy and the myth of American exceptionalism are often the culprits, as is so with many injustices in the past and present narrative of this country. And that erasure starts in our formative years.

Julian Hayter, a historian and associate professor at the University of Richmond in Virginia, told NBC News that school curriculum "was never designed to be anything other than white supremacist, and it has been very difficult to convince people that other versions of history are not only worth telling. They're absolutely essential for us as a country to move closer to something that might reflect reconciliation but even more importantly, the truth." LaGarrett King, who is an associate professor of social studies education at the University of Missouri, as well as founding director of the institution's Carter Center for K–12 Black History Education, agreed: "Really, the overarching theme is, 'Yes, we made mistakes, but we overcame because we are the United States of America.' What that has done is it has erased tons of history that would combat that progressive narrative. So, of course you're not going to have crucial information such as what happened in Tulsa."

While the massacre claimed so many lives, their legacy and the stories of the survivors will not be forgotten—the stories of Americans who lived through beautiful times and horrific times, which is the story of America itself. And now it is up to each one of us to ensure their stories continue to be told. As the courageous journalist, anti-lynching activist, and civil rights pioneer Ida B. Wells-Barnett wrote, "The way to right wrongs is to turn the light of truth upon them."

Afterword

Much like it was truly eye-opening to write about an event that happened one hundred years ago, and everything that led up to it, I can't imagine what historians will think when they write about 2020 decades from now. I was researching and writing *Black Birds in the Sky* during a tumultuous year, as life changed right before our collective eyes. Yet one aspect I was struck by is how very little things seem to have actually changed between previous centuries and the time I was living through. Or, rather, how many harmful elements of US politics and culture have endured despite the progress we have achieved.

In 1918, the world was hit with a new and deadly strain of influenza. Per the Centers for Disease Control and Prevention, "with no vaccine to protect against influenza infection and no antibiotics to treat secondary bacterial infections that can be associated with influenza infections, control efforts world-wide were limited to non-pharmaceutical interventions such as isolation, quarantine, good personal hygiene, use of disinfectants, and limitations of public gatherings, which were applied unevenly." Sound familiar?

As of this writing in February 2021, the United States had exceeded 27 million infections of the novel coronavirus (COVID-19) and had reported more than 460,000 deaths. Living under some form of safer-at-home or stay-at-home orders since March 2020—the same month the World Health Organization declared a global pandemic—many Americans have been endlessly vocal about how these deaths could have been prevented, if only more people would adhere to wearing masks in public, practice social distancing and give up large group gatherings, and wash their hands. Many more place the blame on President Donald J. Trump, who early on ignored hard science while spreading lies about the disease's deadliness and infection rate, and publicly shunned the most basic advice of health professionals.

Still, an equally loud group felt their freedom was being threatened by being asked to take measures that help keep others safe, including those at greater risk of contracting and dying from disease: those with health conditions, the poor, the elderly, and communities of color.

And none of this was new.

During the 1918 pandemic, President Woodrow Wilson—the same guy who screened *The Birth of a Nation* in the White House and was reported to have wholeheartedly agreed with the portrayal of the KKK as heroes—severely mishandled the governmental response to the new strain of flu, which ended up killing an estimated 675,000 Americans in fifteen months and at least 50 million people worldwide. According to historian John M. Barry, "Wilson never made a public statement about the pandemic. Never." And, just as President Trump reportedly contracted COVID-19, Wilson came down with the very virus he had refused to acknowledge to the people he was supposed to be leading. Many people around him were infected with the virus as well, same as the Trump administration, their families, and the people who worked for them.

Without effective national leadership, cities and states were primarily left to the whims of their mayors and governors, and the numbers showed exactly how that played out. Philadelphia's leaders refused to cancel a World War I parade in September 1918, despite widespread evidence of the flu's deadliness, and more than twelve thousand people died in just a few weeks, first overcrowding hospitals and then overwhelming the city's morgues.

St. Louis, on the other hand, which was the sixth-largest US city at the time, "was very quick to implement city closures," J. Alexander Navarro, assistant director for the Center for the History of Medicine at the University of Michigan, told *USA Today*. He said Dr. Max Starkloff, the city's "energetic and visionary" health commissioner, helped usher in lifesaving health protocols, by closing public gathering spaces, such as schools, theaters, and churches, and banning group activities altogether—including St. Louis's own war parade. Records show that between September and December 1918, Philadelphia saw nearly fourteen thousand deaths from the virus, while St. Louis recorded just under three thousand.

The viral natures of the 1918 influenza strain and COVID-19 aren't identical, but the safeguards suggested by scientists are similar enough to see that many deaths in both cases were easily preventable. Yet some politicians and citizens alike continue to disregard science and professional advice in favor of exercising their "freedom."

One question I keep coming back to as I think about these two deadly pandemics: Is history bound to repeat itself no matter what, or does it repeat itself because so many people don't want to look to the past to see how we got to the future?

As the pandemic swept news cycles across the world in March 2020, little national attention was given to the murder of Breonna Taylor, a twenty-six-year-old Black medical worker in Kentucky, who was shot and killed in her bed by a white Louisville Metro Police officer on March 13 during what several sources have described as a "botched" raid. Nor were people talking about Ahmaud Arbery, a twenty-five-year-old Black man who, a few weeks earlier, had been stalked and murdered by two armed white men in south Georgia for the apparent crime of jogging while Black.

Arbery's death began making national headlines in April 2020, after video was released and activists began to speak up; his killers were finally charged on May 7—more than two months after Arbery's murder. Meanwhile, Taylor's story didn't receive the attention it deserved until May 2020—the same month her family filed a wrongful death lawsuit against the Louisville Metro officers. The national coverage lit a fire under the city's law enforcement: Louisville's FBI office finally opened an investigation on May 21; the same day, the Louisville Metro Police Department announced its officers would be required to wear body cameras moving forward.

These deaths of innocent Black people would be unjust at any time, but they felt particularly egregious as the country struggled with the pandemic, which was endangering health, jobs, and food security. Add to this the fact that Black people and other communities of color were more likely to contract and die from COVID-19 due to housing conditions, working in essential jobs, and inadequate access to health care, and tensions grew incredibly high.

Then came Memorial Day.

In New York City, Black birdwatcher Christian Cooper began his morning in the Ramble, a "woodland retreat" in Central Park where he was looking for songbirds. When he asked a white woman in the area named Amy Cooper (no relation) to follow the park rules and leash her dog, she called the police on him, telling him she was going to report that "an African American man is threatening my life." Video evidence showed Christian posed no threat and kept his distance from Amy. But her whole demeanor changed as she spoke to the 911 dispatcher, shrieking that she was in danger. It was later revealed that in a second conversation with a 911 operator, she'd claimed Christian had assaulted her. Amy Cooper was confident that her word would be believed over his because she was aware of the history in this country—that in cases like this one, white women are always the victims, and Black men are always the aggressors. She threatened *his* life by calling law enforcement because she knew the police would likely believe her word over his. In this instance, however, she was wrong. After admitting that he had not threatened her life or assaulted her, Amy Cooper was charged with a misdemeanor for filing a false police report; she was also fired from her job.

Although Amy Cooper was held accountable for actions that she very well knew were endangering Christian Cooper's life, the echoes of Black men being lynched over false accusations from white women were all too clear.

Just a few hours later, in Minneapolis, Minnesota, forty-six-year-old George Floyd, an unarmed Black man, was arrested after allegedly trying to pay for cigarettes with a fake twenty-dollar bill. Responding to a call, a white Minneapolis police officer pinned Floyd to the pavement and kneeled on his neck for more than nine minutes, rendering Floyd, who begged for his life, unconscious. Multiple witnesses watched him die under the officer's knee. Because it was caught on video, the world watched as well.

Everyone has their breaking point, and this holds true with communities, too. Watching yet another Black person die at the hands of the police, and a white woman recklessly calling law enforcement because she didn't like being asked by a Black man to follow the rules—all in a year that was already fraught with so much unnecessary death and financial hardship—was too much to bear. And, once again, the people took to the streets.

But this time felt different. The murders of Trayvon Martin in 2012, Michael Brown in 2014, John Crawford in 2014, Tamir Rice in 2014, Eric Garner in 2014, Samuel DuBose in 2015, Freddie Gray in 2015, Sandra Bland in 2015, Walter Scott in 2015, Terence Crutcher in 2016, Alton Sterling in 2016, Philando Castile in 2016, Jordan Edwards in 2017, Stephon Clark in 2018, Elijah McClain in 2019, and Atatiana Jefferson in 2019 were well documented and protested. And yet the protests that emerged after Floyd's death felt monumental.

The *New York Times* reported that "within 24 hours of Mr. Floyd's death, demonstrations were organized in a half-dozen US cities, with protesters chanting the names of Black people subjected to police brutality." The protesters were not just Black or people of color this time. Scores of white people joined in, too—many of them who, despite the list of police brutality victims in the previous paragraph, had just woken up to the very real problem of the unequal treatment of Black people in the United States. The protests grew, stretching to "more than 2,000 cities and towns," and eventually going global as crowds of masked people insisted Black Lives Matter.

I had always heard that modern-day police departments were rooted in slave patrols, yet I was still surprised by the clear connection in my research. Many, many police officers set out each day to do their job of protecting the people they serve and would never think of shooting, let alone killing, an unarmed person simply because the sight of Black or brown skin made them "fear for their lives." But it's hard to divorce the way in which slave patrols in the South targeted Black people before slavery was abolished from the way in which police departments, their reorganized reincarnations, did afterward. To these forces, Black people were always the enemy—a community to be "tamed," whose mere existence presents a threat to the maintenance of the status quo—and those ideals have clearly persisted through generations of law enforcement who failed to see Black people as free, equal, and worthy of living their lives unbothered.

As if rapidly mounting deaths from the pandemic, and killings of Black Americans at the hands of police weren't enough, 2020 was also a presidential election year in the United States.

With a country growing increasingly divided, due in large part to divisive leadership, few people were looking forward to an election cycle that would have been stressful even under normal circumstances. And as the campaigns kicked off in earnest, President Trump announced his decision to hold his first public rally after the onset of the pandemic in Tulsa, Oklahoma, on June 19—otherwise known as Juneteenth. Although it is not yet established as a national holiday, many states recognize and commemorate Juneteenth as an observance of June 19, 1865, the date upon which Union soldiers traveled to Galveston, Texas, to inform the state's two hundred fifty thousand enslaved people that they were free—more than two and a half years after President Lincoln issued the Emancipation Proclamation. Celebrations include a variety of activities such as barbecues and rodeos, and red foods such as watermelon, hot links, red velvet cake, and red soda are often served.

Trump's plan to hold a rally on the commemoration of this historic day was met with widespread opposition, to say the least.

Attorney, poet, and educator CeLillianne Green told the *Washington Post* the Trump campaign's decision was "almost blasphemous to the people of Tulsa and insulting to the notion of freedom for our people, which is what Juneteenth symbolizes. I'm speechless. That day is the day those people in Texas found out they were free. The juxtaposition of the massacre of Black people and Juneteenth, the delayed notice you are free, is outrageous. Juneteenth symbolized our freedom."

Trump denied he purposely set the Tulsa rally on June 19, but a couple of days later, he announced the date would be changed.

To list the entirety of what I consider to be harmful policies and errors in judgment enacted by this president would take more space than I am allowed here, and is not necessarily energy I feel would be useful for this book. But again, as I researched Reconstruction, the years after the Civil War ended, I was struck by Trump's similarities to Andrew Johnson, who stepped into the presidency after Lincoln was assassinated. And I wasn't alone in noticing this; countless articles have been written about the parallels between the two men, whose presidential terms took place more than 150 years apart.

In an article for the *New York Times*, Professor Manisha Sinha wrote: "Both Johnson's and Mr. Trump's concept of American nationalism is narrow, parochial, and authoritarian.

Johnson opposed the 14th Amendment, ratified in 1868, that guarantees equality before the law to all persons and citizenship to all born in the United States. Mr. Trump has threatened both to revoke its constitutional guarantee of national birthright citizenship and have the entire amendment overturned." And in a short list of presidential impeachments, Johnson was the first president to be impeached, while Trump is the most recent (though Johnson was impeached only once).

In addition to both presidents pardoning people who committed unpatriotic crimes (Confederate generals and white people who murdered Black people in Johnson's case, a Navy SEAL "who violated the military's rules of conduct" in Trump's); Johnson's "rambling, drunken" speech as he took the oath of office for the vice presidency and Trump's "presidential campaign full of grotesque insults, ridicule, lies, and vulgarity"; and both "engag[ing] in actions that have dangerous repercussions for American democracy"; Sinha went on to note that "most significantly, both men made an undisguised championship of white supremacy . . . and played on the politics of racial division."

The stress of the 2020 election was further compounded by the still-raging pandemic; as the deaths continued to mount, Americans had to decide whether they should risk voting in person or use mail-in or drop-off ballots. And, in the months leading up to the election, the Trump administration and pro-Trump Republicans did their best to undermine the voting system, hearkening back to the voter suppression tactics that have run rampant in past decades across the United States, but most egregiously in the South.

Election Day turned into Election Week as states worked hard to count an unprecedented number of votes; according to the *Washington Post*, "More Americans voted in the 2020 election—two-thirds of the voting eligible population—than in any other in 120 years." This record voter turnout was in large part due to the tireless efforts of Black women activists and politicians like Stacey Abrams, whose years of dedication to fair elections resulted in flipping several states from Republican in 2016 to Democrat in 2020, along with turning the Senate from majority-Republican to majority-Democrat in a historic runoff election in January 2021. However, though Joseph Biden—whose running mate, Kamala Harris, is the first woman, Black woman, and woman of Indian descent to serve as vice president—received eighty-one million votes, the most of any presidential candidate ever, the election was close. Nearly 47 percent of the country, or more than seventy-four million Americans, voted for Donald Trump.

As the days of Trump's presidency were coming to an end, many of his supporters refused to accept the fact that he had lost the election—a refusal that was directly attributed to his own unsubstantiated claims that he had won the election and that Americans around the country had engaged in voter fraud that resulted in Biden's win. And with the encouragement of senators such as Josh Hawley (who represents my home state of Missouri) and Ted Cruz from Texas, thousands of these supporters stormed the US Capitol Building in Washington, DC, on January 6, 2021, to overturn the presidential election results, or "stop the steal." Bearing guns, tear gas, police restraints, and zip ties, among other weapons and occupation gear, the primarily white mob hung a noose in front of the building, damaged federal property, and burst into the Senate chamber, forcing members of Congress to go on lockdown. Whatever it was that happened—a failed coup d'état? An insurrection? A good old-fashioned riot?—Americans watched in horror as Trump supporters attacked the Capitol, leaving at least five people dead, including a Capitol police officer.

Many of them wondered: Where was law enforcement? After all, peaceful Black Lives Matter activists protesting on the steps of the Lincoln Memorial in June 2020 had been met by a wall of armed and uniformed National Guard members. In the immediate aftermath of the Capitol riot, video emerged of police officers taking selfies with rioters, and appearing to open barricades, established to prevent precisely this sort of unauthorized access, to people who would threaten the legislative branch of government. And, at the time of this writing, dozens of off-duty police officers and public officials from around the country have been questioned or arrested in connection with the attack on the Capitol—and investigations are still ongoing.

On January 13, one week before he was set to leave office, Trump became the first president to be impeached twice—this time for "inciting violence against the government of the United States." For history buffs, the events of January 6 brought to mind the meticulously planned 1898 insurrection, or massacre, in Wilmington, North Carolina, in which an armed mob of white supremacists overthrew their local government, which included Black and white politicians; burned down the office of Black newspaper the *Daily Record*; and murdered dozens of Black people. The mob was never punished, and for decades, their actions were attributed to a "race riot," which the Black people they'd terrorized were accused of instigating.

In the days after Biden was named president-elect, many people wondered how so many Americans—nearly enough to give Trump a second term—were willing to vote for someone who had done so much to damage the country's democracy, reputation, and integrity.

I personally believe much of it is because Americans don't know their history. Results from a fifty-state survey released in September 2020 showed that 63 percent of Gen Z and millennial respondents didn't know that six million Jewish people had been killed in the Holocaust, and 36 percent believed "two million or fewer" were murdered. According to the Claims Conference, "In perhaps one of the most disturbing revelations of this survey, 11 percent of U.S. Millennial and Gen Z respondents believe Jews caused the Holocaust." Of the survey respondents, 48 percent couldn't name a single concentration camp or ghetto in Europe during the Holocaust.

This is abhorrent and extremely upsetting, especially coupled with the high percentage of respondents who had encountered Holocaust denial on social media—the same social media sites on which President Trump incited violence from his supporters, and from which he was broadly banned in January 2021. For a horror like the Holocaust to be denied or widely unknown just seventy-five years after the largest Nazi concentration camp, Auschwitz, was liberated, is unfathomable. And the fact that social media is also partially to blame for disinformation and the growth of hate groups is troubling, considering how big a part it plays in so many of our lives.

But it also helps me see why a tragedy like the Tulsa Race Massacre of 1921 could be so effectively hidden for decades. Trauma is painful. It's difficult to discuss, and often even harder to make sense of. But pretending so-called unspeakable things simply didn't happen is not the way to grow, to become better people or make a better world. Not only is it utterly disrespectful to the people who lost their lives in such genocides, but it is detrimental to the lives and progress of the survivors and their descendants.

I don't like to tell people what to take from my books. I prefer my readers to interpret the words for themselves, to discover the themes and significance through their own reasoning with the information given. But if there is one thing readers take from this book, I hope it is that *history matters*. Stories matter, and it also matters who is telling these stories.

I think about how my parents grew up in a small Arkansas county that had been home to one of the deadliest race massacres in United States history, and how I grew up in a town where a triple lynching had led to the decimation of the Black community decades before I was born, and how for the first twenty-two years of my life, I unknowingly lived three hours away from a neighborhood that was the site of the Tulsa Race Massacre. How could my life, or my ancestors' lives, have been different if just one of those events had turned out differently?

What would this country look like if more Black people grew up being taught their history as much as they are taught the stories of white Americans? How would people interact with one another if white Americans learned early on that they are not the center of every story, or that their stories are not the only ones that matter?

I am haunted by these questions the further I dig into this country's past, but I'm not deterred. And while I hope this book contains some answers about the history of the complex relationship between the United States and Black Americans, I hope it also raises some questions for its readers.

A framed art print hangs in my home that reads ASK MORE QUESTIONS. I've always valued this advice; I see it as a nod to my love of journalism, which I spent four years studying in college. But these words are, first and foremost, a fervent reminder to continue seeking out the truth every day, and to never stop sharing it.

—Brandy Colbert, February 2021

Acknowledgments

Although I have worked in journalism in some capacity for my entire adult life, I never saw myself writing a nonfiction book. I knew as soon as I began talking about *Black Birds in the Sky* that it would be a huge undertaking, but I wasn't prepared for just how rewarding it would be in the end. And, like all of my previous books, I could not have done it without the help of so many dedicated, talented people.

Tina Dubois, this is our seventh book and tenth year of working together. Your belief in and encouragement of my work over the last decade has been so deeply meaningful. Thank you for being such a fierce advocate of my writing and a wonderful friend to me.

Jordan Brown! I so admire your big brain and big heart, and I'm incredibly grateful for the work you've put into this book. Thank you for your insight, smart questions, and precise edits that made me feel confident I dug as deep as possible when it was possible. I'm proud to have worked on this with you.

And to the rest of the team at Balzer + Bray/HarperCollins, especially Alessandra Balzer, Donna Bray, Tiara Kittrell, Alison Donalty, Mark Rifkin, Josh Weiss, Nellie Kurtzman, Shannon Cox, Audrey Diestelkamp, Aubrey Churchward, Patty Rosati, and Victor Hendrickson, thank you for everything you've done for me and this book. It's an honor to work with such a terrific group of people.

Corina Lupp and Natasha Cunningham, thank you for

honoring *Black Birds in the Sky* with such a beautiful, evocative cover. Shona McCarthy, Erica Ferguson, and Megan Gendell, I am also a copy editor and fact-checker, and I could not have asked for a better team to work on this book. I'm forever grateful for the meticulous care and respect you showed for every sentence.

Thank you to Luke Williams, archivist and curator of collections at the Tulsa Historical Society, for working so efficiently to help us obtain the bulk of the photos for this book.

Harry Gamble, thank you for helping me understand the beauty in learning about the past. You're a raconteur of the highest order and your spontaneous stories during our workdays all those years ago in Chicago made me realize just how compelling history can be.

I'm indebted to several writers and historians whose work immensely aided my research, particularly Scott Ellsworth, Eddie Faye Gates, and Hannibal B. Johnson. The "Tulsa Race Riot: A Report by the Oklahoma Commission to Study the Tulsa Race Riot of 1921" and the Oklahoma Historical Society site were especially helpful in crafting large sections of this book.

And, finally, I'm thankful to my family, particularly my parents, for always telling me the truth about where we come from. Even when the memories are uncomfortable to revisit. I am grateful for your stories and your love.

Source List and Image Credits

Foreword

4: "one of the worst episodes of racial violence in American history": Nan Elizabeth Woodruff, "The Forgotten History of America's Worst Racial Massacre," *New York Times*, September 30, 2019, www.nytimes.com/2019/09/30/opinion/elaine-massacre-1919-arkansas.html.

6–9: 1906 triple lynching in Springfield: Jenny Fillmer, "1906 Lynchings Grew from Tensions, Racism—Thriving Black Community Died," *Springfield News-Leader*, April 14, 2006, www.news-leader.com/story/news/local/ozarks/2006/04/14/1906-lynchings-grew-from-tensions-racism-thriving-black-community-died/77385626.

10: August 2002 plaque: Associated Press, "Springfield Installs Plaque Remembering Lynchings," *Southeast Missourian*, August 5, 2002, www.semissourian.com/story/83976.html.

10: Thomas Gilyard memorial: Ines Kagubare, "Truth and Reconciliation Sought as Joplin Lynching Recalled," *Joplin Globe*, April 15, 2018, www.joplinglobe.com/news/local_news/truth-and-reconciliation-sought-as-joplin-lynching-recalled/article_282f07b1-1c10-50a8-b589-ecb28e92cbd8.html.

10: October 2019 historical marker: Sara Karnes, "Coalition Unveils Marker for Three Men Lynched at Park Central Square in 1906," *Springfield News-Leader*, October 2, 2019, www.news-leader.com/story/news/local/ozarks/2019/10/02/springfield-missouri-lynching-park-central-square-memorial/3829563002.

May 30, 1921

12: Genevieve Elizabeth Tillman Jackson quote: "Meet the Survivors," Greenwood Cultural Center, John Hope Franklin Center for Reconciliation, www.jhfcenter.org/1921-race-massacre-survivors.

12: image: Tulsa Historical Society & Museum

13–16: Dick Rowland / Jimmie Jones background: Tim Madigan, *The Burning: Massacre, Destruction, and the Tulsa Race Riot of 1921* (New York: Thomas Dunne Books, 2001), 47–49.

14–15: *Plessy v. Ferguson*: Judgment decided May 18, 1896; Records of the Supreme Court of the United States; Record Group 267; *Plessy v. Ferguson*, 163, #15248, National Archives. www.ourdocuments.gov/doc.php?flash=false&doc=52.

1. Oklahoma! Soon Be Livin' in a Brand-New State

18: Beulah Lane Keenan Smith quote: "Meet the Survivors," Greenwood Cultural Center, John Hope Franklin Center for Reconciliation, www.jhfcenter.org/1921-race-massacre-survivors.

18: image: Tulsa Historical Society & Museum

22: Andrew Jackson enslaved about 150 people: DeNeen L. Brown, "Hunting Down Runaway Slaves: The Cruel Ads of Andrew Jackson and 'the Master Class,'" *Washington Post*, May 1, 2017, www.washingtonpost.com/news/retropolis/wp/2017/04/11/hunting-down-runaway-slaves-the-cruel-ads-of-andrew-jackson-and-the-master-class.

23, 25: "the Indian problem" and "a trail of tears and death": "Trail of Tears," History.com, updated July 7, 2020, www.history.com/topics/native-american-history/trail-of-tears.

25: image: NPS.gov

26: "celebrate the Mvskoke (Muscogee) people": "Where It All Began: Muscogee (Creek) Nation Reflects Arrival to Indian Territory, History of Council Oak Tree," Muscogee (Creek) Nation, October 24, 2018, www.mcn-nsn.gov/reflects-arrival-to-indian-territory -history-of-council-oak-tree.

30: "I salute Kentucky Daisey's claim!": Stan Hoig, "Daisey, Nanitta R. H.," *The Encyclopedia of Oklahoma History and Culture*, www.okhistory.org/publications/enc/entry .php?entry=DA004.

33: The Curtis Act: M. Kaye Tatro, "Curtis Act (1898)," *The Encyclopedia of Oklahoma History and Culture*, www.okhistory.org/publications/enc/entry.php?entry=CU006.

35–36: Jim Crow laws: "Jim Crow Laws in Oklahoma," Oklahoman, February 13, 2005, www.oklahoman.com/article/2884332/jim-crow-laws-in-oklahoma.

36–38: Cherokee Nation enslavers / Slave Revolt of 1842: Art T. Burton, "Slave Revolt of 1842," *The Encyclopedia of Oklahoma History and Culture*, www.okhistory.org/publications /enc/entry.php?entry=SL002.

39: Black Boomers: Ron Jackson, "Blacks among Boomers," *Oklahoman*, February 18, 2001, www.oklahoman.com/article/2730943/blacks-among-boomers.

2. To Be Black in America

42: Julius Warren Scott quote: "Meet the Survivors," Greenwood Cultural Center, John Hope Franklin Center for Reconciliation, www.jhfcenter.org/1921-race-massacre -survivors.

42: image: Tulsa Historical Society & Museum

44: "banned by the government": "Black Soldiers in the U.S. Military During the Civil War," National Archives, September 1, 2017, www.archives.gov/education/lessons/blacks -civil-war.

46: Frederick Douglass on Andrew Johnson: Frederick Douglass, *The Life and Times of Frederick Douglass* (Mineola, New York: Dover Publications, 2003), 264.

47: "a country for white men": Hans L. Trefousse, *Andrew Johnson, A Biography* (New York: W. W. Norton and Company, 1989), 236.

49: image: National Portrait Gallery, Smithsonian Institution

58: Oregon passes "lash law," bans Black people: "African Americans on the Oregon Trail," National Park Service, updated February 1, 2021, www.nps.gov/articles/000 /african-americans-on-the-oregon-trail.htm.

58: "full KKK regalia": Tim Winkle, "When Watchmen Were Klansmen," National Museum of American History (Kenneth E. Behring Center) blog, April 28, 2020, www .americanhistory.si.edu/blog/watchmen.

59: Oklahoma lynchings: Dianna Everett, "Lynching," *The Encyclopedia of Oklahoma History and Culture*, www.okhistory.org/publications/enc/entry.php?entry=LY001.

60: "Whites could not countenance": Philip Dray, *At the Hands of Persons Unknown: The Lynching of Black America* (New York: The Modern Library, 2003), 64.

60: "lynch a thousand a week": "Felton, Rebecca Latimer," History, Art & Archives: United States House of Representatives, May 2, 2021, https://history.house.gov/People/Listing/F /FELTON,-Rebecca-Latimer-(F000069).

62: image: National Portrait Gallery, Smithsonian Institution

63: "one lone Negro": Ida B. Wells, *Crusade for Justice* (Chicago: University of Chicago Press, 1970), 316.

64–66: Roy Belton lynching: "Tulsa Race Riot: A Report by the Oklahoma Commission to Study the Tulsa Race Riot of 1921," February 28, 2001; Scott Ellsworth, *Death in a Promised Land: The Tulsa Race Riot of 1921* (Baton Rouge: Louisiana State University Press, 1982), 50–53.

3. Fighting for Survival

71: "The world must be made safe for democracy": "Echoes of the Great War: American Experiences of World War I," Library of Congress, www.loc.gov/exhibitions/world-war -i-american-experiences/about-this-exhibition/arguing-over-war/for-or-against-war /wilson-before-congress.

72: "poor and inadequate": Jami L. Bryan, "Fighting for Respect: African-American Soldiers in World War I," Army Historical Foundation, www.armyhistory.org/fighting-for -respect-african-american-soldiers-in-wwi.

74: "first major race riot of the World War I period": Olivia B. Waxman, "The Forgotten March That Started the National Civil Rights Movement Took Place 100 Years Ago," *Time*, updated August 18, 2020, www.time.com/4828991/east-saint-louis-riots-1917.

76: image: Underwood Archives/Getty Images

79: "Lincoln freed you," "no-gooders": Harper Barnes, *Never Been a Time: The 1917 Race Riot That Sparked the Civil Rights Movement* (New York: Walker, 2008).

79–80: National Association for the Advancement of Colored People mission: "About the NAACP," www.naacp.org/about-us.

79: image: National Portrait Gallery, Smithsonian Institution

80: "If it goes unchallenged": Dorian Lynskey, "A Public Menace: How the Fight to Ban *The Birth of a Nation* Shaped the Nascent Civil Rights Movement," *Slate*, March 31, 2015, www.slate.com/culture/2015/03/the-birth-of-a-nation-how-the-fight-to-censor-d-w -griffiths-film-shaped-american-history.html.

81: "'Bring your gun home'": Alexander DeConde, *Gun Violence in America: The Struggle for Control* (Boston: Northeastern University Press, 2001), 73.

82–84: "One Florida law" / "Impress the Negro" / Daniel Mack: Equal Justice Initiative, "Lynching in America: Targeting Black Veterans," 2017.

88: "round up" / "heavily armed" / "insurrection": Francine Uenuma, "The Massacre of Black Sharecroppers That Led the Supreme Court to Curb the Racial Disparities of the Justice System," *Smithsonian Magazine*, August 2, 2018, www.smithsonianmag.com /history/death-hundreds-elaine-massacre-led-supreme-court-take-major-step-toward -equal-justice-african-americans-180969863.

May 31, 1921

90: B. C. Franklin quote: Buck Colbert Franklin, "Read an Eyewitness Account of the Massacre That Opens *Watchmen*," *Slate*, October 23, 2019, www.slate.com/culture/2019/10 /watchmen-b-c-franklin-tulsa-massacre-account-full-text.html.

90: image: Tulsa Historical Society & Museum

95: image: Map from "Tulsa Race Riot: A Report by the Oklahoma Commission to Study the Tulsa Race Riot of 1921."

97 / 100: "came back from France" / "the race war was on": Scott Ellsworth, *Death in a Promised Land: The Tulsa Race Riot of 1921* (Baton Rouge: Louisiana State University Press, 1982), 109, 61.

All other quotes: "Tulsa Race Riot: A Report by the Oklahoma Commission to Study the Tulsa Race Riot of 1921," February 28, 2001.

4. Black Wall Street Comes Alive

102: Delois Vaden Ramsey quote: "Meet the Survivors," Greenwood Cultural Center, John Hope Franklin Center for Reconciliation, www.jhfcenter.org/1921-race-massacre-survivors.

102: image: Tulsa Historical Society & Museum

108: image: Tulsa Historical Society & Museum

109: "lined up waiting": "Tulsa Race Riot: A Report by the Oklahoma Commission to Study the Tulsa Race Riot of 1921," February 28, 2001.

110: "colorful, flamboyant," "a smooth talker": Carlos Moreno, "The Victory of Greenwood: Simon Berry," *Tulsa Star*, August 23, 2020, www.newtulsastar.com/2020/08/23/the-victory-of-greenwood-simon-berry.

110: "the first Black woman millionaire in America": "Madam C. J. Walker," History.com, updated January 26, 2021, www.history.com/topics/black-history/madame-c-j-walker.

111: "the promised land": Pete Earley, "The Untold Story of One of America's Worst Race Riots," *Washington Post*, September 12, 1982, www.washingtonpost.com/archive/opinions/1982/09/12/the-untold-story-of-one-of-americas-worst-race-riots/e37fc963-71dd-45cc-8cb0-04ab8032bcd2.

113: image: Ruth Sigler Avery Collection-Tulsa Race Massacre of 1921, Department of Special Collections and Archives, Oklahoma State University-Tulsa

114: "the most able Negro surgeon in America" / "not a decent living": Ellsworth, *Death in a Promised Land*, 67, 10.

5. Extra! Extra! Read All About It!, or the Promise of a Lynching

118: Johnnie L. Grayson Brown quote: "Meet the Survivors," Greenwood Cultural Center, John Hope Franklin Center for Reconciliation, www.jhfcenter.org/1921-race-massacre-survivors.

118: image: Tulsa Historical Society & Museum

120: "the most important Black journalist": Henry Louis Gates Jr., "What Was the 1st Black American Newspaper?," *The Root*, March 10, 2014, www.theroot.com/what-was-the-1st-black-american-newspaper-1790874894.

122: "the land of their fathers," "unfavorable to": "Africans in America: The American Colonization Society," PBS, www.pbs.org/wgbh/aia/part3/3p1521.html.

126: image: Tulsa Historical Society & Museum

129: "single most important force": Scott Ellsworth, *Death in a Promised Land: The Tulsa Race Riot of 1921* (Baton Rouge: Louisiana State University Press, 1982), 110.

130–131: "only bylined story" / "Without pausing": Randy Krehbiel, "Tulsa Race Massacre: 1921 Tulsa Newspapers Fueled Racism, and One Story Is Cited for Sparking Greenwood's Burning," *Tulsa World*, May 31, 2019, www.tulsaworld.com/news/tulsa-race-massacre-1921-tulsa-newspapers-fueled-racism-and-one-story-is-cited-for-sparking/article_420593ee-8090-5cfc-873e-d2dd26d2054e.html.

June 1, 1921

134: Ernestine Gibbs quote: "Meet the Survivors," Greenwood Cultural Center, John Hope Franklin Center for Reconciliation, www.jhfcenter.org/1921-race-massacre-survivors.

134: image: Tulsa Historical Society & Museum

136: "not a damn one": Scott Ellsworth, *Death in a Promised Land: The Tulsa Race Riot of 1921* (Baton Rouge: Louisiana State University Press, 1982), 63.

140–141: "but my mother witnessed": Hannibal B. Johnson, *Black Wall Street: From Riot to Renaissance in Tulsa's Historic Greenwood District* (Fort Worth, Texas: Eakin Press, 1998), 68.

141–142, 146: B. C. Franklin quotes: Buck Colbert Franklin, "Read an Eyewitness Account of the Massacre That Opens *Watchmen*," *Slate*, October 23, 2019, www.slate.com/culture/2019/10/watchmen-b-c-franklin-tulsa-massacre-account-full-text.html.

143, 144, 147: images: Tulsa Historical Society & Museum

148, 149–150: "I had gone to bed" / "I remember we hid": Johnson, *Black Wall Street*, 67, 76.

All other direct quotes: "Tulsa Race Riot: A Report by the Oklahoma Commission to Study the Tulsa Race Riot of 1921," February 28, 2001.

6. The Aftermath

152: Simon R. Richardson quote: "Meet the Survivors," Greenwood Cultural Center, John Hope Franklin Center for Reconciliation, www.jhfcenter.org/1921-race-massacre-survivors.

152: image: Tulsa Historical Society & Museum

153–154: James T. West quotes: Scott Ellsworth, *Death in a Promised Land: The Tulsa Race Riot of 1921* (Baton Rouge: Louisiana State University Press, 1982), 81.

154, 156: images: Tulsa Historical Society & Museum

156–157: J. W. Hughes quotes: Hannibal B. Johnson, *Black Wall Street: From Riot to Renaissance in Tulsa's Historic Greenwood District* (Fort Worth, Texas: Eakin Press, 1998), 66.

157: Mary Elizabeth Jones Parrish quote: Ellsworth, *Death in a Promised Land*, 112.

159: "some bodies": Johnson, *Black Wall Street*, 139.

159: image: Tulsa Historical Society & Museum

160: "decent burials" / grand jury report excerpt: Ellsworth, *Death in a Promised Land*, 79, 105.

162: "those employed regularly": Ellsworth, *Death in a Promised Land*, 82.

162: "dereliction of duty": Randy Krehbiel, "Tulsa Race Massacre: In Aftermath, No One Prosecuted for Killings, and Insurance Claims Were Rejected but Greenwood Persevered," *Tulsa World*, May 31, 2020, www.tulsaworld.com/news/local/racemassacre/tulsa-race-massacre-in-aftermath-no-one-prosecuted-for-killings-and-insurance-claims-were-rejected/article_3ba23c3c-886d-5821-9970-02153261960a.html.

164: image: Tulsa Historical Society & Museum

165: "written request of Page": Randy Krehbiel, "Tulsa Race Massacre: What Happened to Sarah Page and Dick Rowland Following the Massacre?" *Tulsa World*, May 31, 2020, www .tulsaworld.com/tulsa-race-massacre-what-happened-to-sarah-page-and-dick-rowland -following-the-massacre/article_67810913-0f34-58da-af38-f6a9ff8ea5e0.html.

7. The Legacy of Greenwood

166: Reverend Dr. Robert Turner quote: Maria Cramer, "Tulsa Massacre Survivors Sue City Nearly 100 Years After Attack," *New York Times*, September 1, 2020, www.nytimes .com/2020/09/01/us/tulsa-race-massacre-lawsuit.html.

166 image: Tulsa Historical Society & Museum

167: "horror," "disgrace,": "Tulsa Race Riot: A Report by the Oklahoma Commission to Study the Tulsa Race Riot of 1921," February 28, 2001.

168: image: Tulsa Historical Society & Museum

170, 172: All quotes: "Tulsa Race Riot: A Report by the Oklahoma Commission."

173: image: Tulsa Historical Society & Museum

175: "historical significance": "History," Tulsa Public Schools: Booker T. Washington High School, www.btw.tulsaschools.org/about-us/history.

175: "fighting for": *Oklahoma Eagle*, "Our Story," theoklahomaeagle.net/about.

176–177: Michael Reed and John Gant quotes: Joseph Holloway, "Black Wall Street Plaques Tell the Story before Tulsa Race Massacre," News on 6, August 27, 2020, www .newson6.com/story/5f4883594552fb4a5a2f3b82/black-wall-street-plaques-tell-the-story -before-tulsa-race-massacre.

179: "plaintiffs neither allege": Chris Casteel and Jay Marks, "Race-Riot Recourse Blocked: Supreme Court Refuses Appeal after Decisions," *Oklahoman*, May 17, 2005, www .oklahoman.com/article/2896719/race-riot-recourse-blocked-br-supreme-court-refuses -appeal-after-decisions.

180: image: Win McNamee/Getty Images

181: All quotes: "Tulsa Race Riot: A Report by the Oklahoma Commission."

181–182: Susan Savage claim / G. T. Bynum quote: DeNeen L. Brown, "Tulsa Mayor Reopens Investigation into Possible Mass Graves from 1921 Race Massacre," *Washington Post*, October 3, 2018, www.washingtonpost.com/local/tulsa-mayor-reopens-investigation -into-possible-mass-graves-from-1921-race-massacre/2018/10/02/df713c96-c68f-11e8 -b2b5-79270f9cce17_story.html.

182: "unearthed eleven coffins," "mass grave": Ben Fenwick, "Mass Grave Unearthed in Tulsa During Search for Massacre Victims," *New York Times*, October 21, 2020, www .nytimes.com/2020/10/21/us/tulsa-massacre-coffins-grave.html.

184: "with the support": Allison Keyes, "A Long-Lost Manuscript Contains a Searing Eyewitness Account of the Tulsa Race Massacre of 1921," *Smithsonian Magazine*, May 27, 2016, www.smithsonianmag.com/smithsonian-institution/long-lost-manuscript-contains -searing-eyewitness-account-tulsa-race-massacre-1921-180959251.

185: "leverage the history": Senator Kevin L. Matthews, "Tulsa Triumphs," 1921 Tulsa Race Massacre Centennial Commission, www.tulsa2021.org/our-vision.

185: "enhance the quality": "Sherry Gamble-Smith and the Black Wall Street Chamber of Commerce," *Black Wall Street Times*, September 9, 2019, www.theblackwallsttimes .com/2019/09/09/sherry-gamble-smith-and-the-black-wall-street-chamber-of -commerce.

186: "eyewitness accounts": "Gilcrease Museum to Receive Eddie Faye Gates Tulsa Race Massacre Collection," *Black Wall Street Times*, updated January 12, 2021, www .theblackwallsttimes.com/2020/10/13/gilcrease-museum-to-receive-eddie-faye-gates-tulsa -race-massacre-collection.

186: "became her mission" / "create resources": James D. Watts Jr., "Eddie Faye Gates' Collection of Race Massacre History Donated to Gilcrease Museum," *Tulsa World*, October 15, 2020, www.tulsaworld.com/entertainment/arts-and-theatre /eddie-faye-gates-collection-of-race-massacre-history-donated-to-gilcrease-museum /article_f5beef58-0d72-11eb-92a2-e7a31274f2eb.html.

187: "Someday": "Timeline: The 1921 Tulsa Race Massacre," *Tulsa World*, May 25, 2020, www.tulsaworld.com/news/local/racemassacre/timeline-the-1921-tulsa-race-massacre /collection_f9a5ed17-68d7-5f6d-921e-8d4207f70d0f.html#1.

187–188: Julian Hayter / LaGarrett King quotes: Daniella Silva, "From Juneteenth to the Tulsa Massacre: What Isn't Taught in Classrooms Has a Profound Effect," NBC News, June 18, 2020, www.nbcnews.com/news/us-news/juneteenth-tulsa-massacre-what-isn-t-taught -classrooms-has-profound-n1231442.

188: "The way to right wrongs": Ida B. Wells, *The Light of Truth: Writings of an Anti-Lynching Crusader* (New York: Penguin Books, 2014), xix.

Afterword

191: "Wilson never": Faith Karimi, "Before Trump Another US President Downplayed a Pandemic and Was Infected," CNN, updated October 3, 2020, www.cnn.com/2020/10/03 /us/woodrow-wilson-coronavirus-trnd/index.html.

191: J. Alexander Navarro quotes: George Petras and Karl Gelles, "100 Years Ago, Philadelphia Chose a Parade over Social Distancing during the 1918 Spanish Flu—and Paid a Heavy Price," *USA Today*, updated May 25, 2020, www.usatoday.com/in-depth /news/2020/05/22/second-wave-coronavirus-spanish-flu-1918-philadelphia-st-louis -influenza-deaths-covid-19/3085405001.

193: "woodland retreat": Central Park Conservancy, "The Ramble," www.centralparknyc .org/locations/the-ramble.

193: "an African-American man": Sarah Maslin Nir, "The Bird Watcher, That Incident and His Feelings on the Woman's Fate," *New York Times*, updated September 9, 2020, www .nytimes.com/2020/05/27/nyregion/amy-cooper-christian-central-park-video.html.

195: All quotes: Audra D. S. Burch, Weiyi Cai, Gabriel Gianordoli, Morrigan McCarthy and Jugal K. Patel, "How Black Lives Matter Reached Every Corner of America," *New York Times*, June 13, 2020, www.nytimes.com/interactive/2020/06/13/us/george-floyd-protests -cities-photos.html.

197: "almost blasphemous": DeNeen L. Brown, "Trump Rally in Tulsa, Site of a Race Massacre, on Juneteenth was 'Almost Blasphemous,' Historian Says," *Washington Post*, June 12, 2020, www.washingtonpost.com/history/2020/06/11/juneteenth-trump-rally -tulsa-race-massacre.

197–198: Johnson/Trump quotes: Manisha Sinha, "Donald Trump, Meet Your Precursor," *New York Times*, November 19, 2019, www.nytimes.com/2019/11/29 /opinion/sunday/andrew-johnson-donald-trump.html.

199: "More Americans": Kevin Schaul, Kate Rabinowitz, and Ted Mellnick, "2020 Turnout Is the Highest in Over a Century," *Washington Post*, updated December 28, 2020, www .washingtonpost.com/graphics/2020/elections/voter-turnout.

200: "inciting violence": Impeaching Donald John Trump, President of the United States, for High Crimes and Misdemeanors, H.R. 24, 117th Cong. (2021), www .congress.gov/bill/117th-congress/house-resolution/24/text.

201: All quotes: "First-Ever 50-State Survey on Holocaust Knowledge of American Millennials and Gen Z Reveals Shocking Results," Claims Conference, September 16, 2020, www.claimscon.org/millennial-study.

Index

abolition, slavery, 43–45, 49–50, 57, 87, 196–97
Alabama, 10, 26, 83, 103, 127
Allen, Will, 6–7, 10
American Colonization Society (ACS), 121–23
Arbery, Ahmaud, 192–93
Arkansas, 4–5, 33, 83, 86–88, 103, 104, 202
Army, US, 71–74, 82–85. *See also* veterans

Bartlesville, Oklahoma, 31–32
Baughman, Theodore, 175
Belton, Roy, 64–66, 92, 94, 96–97, 98–99, 116
Biden, Joseph, 199, 201
The Birth of a Nation (film), 54, 80, 190–91
Black Americans, 52, 57, 178, 192–95, 203. *See also* slavery
Black codes, 35, 47–48, 53, 57, 81–82
Black Dispatch, 131, 137
Black men, 48, 54, 59, 60–61, 72, 78, 79, 83, 85, 88, 89, 96, 97–100, 107, 138, 142, *143*, *144*, 146, 158, *159*, 161, 162, 194–95
Black gun ownership, 81–83, 97–100, 129, 160–62
Black newspapers, 63, 66, 108, 120, 126–29, 131, 175–76, 201
Black Tulsans, 11–13, 66–67, 96–99, 111–112, 115, 117, 127, 130–32, 135, 137–46, 148, 153, *154*, 155, *156*, 162, 163, 165, 168, 178–180, *180*
Black women, 40, 60, 74, 77, 79, 141, 157, 199
Boston, 56, 80, 119–20
Brown, Johnnie L. Grayson, 118
Buckner, Emma, *108*

California, 6, 32, 58, 163
Chandler, Claude, 66–67, 129
Cherokee Nation, 19, 22, 24–26, *25*, 31, 36–38
children, 55, 75, 137, 141, 149–50, 152
Choctaw Nation, 24, 25, 37
citizenship, 22, 32, 45–47, 50, 198
civil rights, 2, 34, 45–47, 80, 173–74
Civil War, 9, 28–29, 35, 38, 43–46, 81, 121
Cleaver, Barney, 97, 99
Coker, Fred, 6–8, 10
Confederate states, 43–45, 48, 50–51, 57

Congress, US, 3, 21, 24, 44–47, *49*, 51, 53, 200
Constitution, US, 44–45, 47, 48, 81, 119–20, 198
Cooper, Christian, 193–94
Cornish, Samuel E., 120–21
COVID-19 pandemic, 190–91, 192, 193

Daisey, Nanitta, 30
deaths, 24–25, 45, 66, 86, 88, 190–95, 198
Tulsa Race Massacre, 137, 144–45, 157–60, 181–82
Democrats, 33–35, 51
Douglass, Frederick, 2, 45–46, 120
Dreamland Theatre, 95–96, 107, 111, 158, *164*, 173, 184
Du Bois, W. E. B., 76, *79*, 79–80, 84
Duncan, Horace B., 6–8, 10

education, 35, 40, 52, 103
Black history in, 1–3, 6, 170–72, 174, 185–88, 203
elevator incident, 16–17, 60, 91–93, 130, 164–65
Ellsworth, Scott, 129, 179
Emancipation Proclamation, 43–44, 45, 196–97

Finley, Robert, 122
fires, 75, 86, 136–37, 141–42, 145–47, *147*, 158
Five Tribes of Oklahoma, 23, 33, 36, 40, 116
Floyd, George, 194–95
Ford, Damie, 14, 15, 16, 91
France, 20, 21, 73–74, 83, 84, 97
Franklin, B. C., 90, 114, 141–42, 146, 173, *173*, 176, 184
Franklin, John Hope, 114, 178, 186–87
freed Black Americans, 38–40, 43–44, 47–51, 57, 105, 121
Freedom's Journal, 120–21
Frisco railroad, Tulsa, 104, 108, 136, 138, *143*

Gates, Eddie Faye, 110, 186
Georgia, 25, 82, 83–84, 192–93
Gibbs, Ernestine, 134
Gill, Loren L., 171, 172
graves, mass, 160, 181–82
Great Migration, 70–71, 74
Greenwood Cultural Center, 177–78, 184
Greenwood District, Tulsa, 11–12, 14–15, 40–41, 90, *95*, 95–100, 178

Black businesses in, 105–12, 137, 176–77
Griffith, D. W., 54
Guinn v. United States, 53, 80
guns, 101, 135–36, 137–39, 142–43, 146, 200
ownership, 81–83, 97–100, 129, 160–62
Gurley, O. W., 14, 97, 103–5, 107, 116
Gustafson, John, 65–66, 98–99, 136, 162

Hamlin, A. C., 51–53
Holocaust, 160, 201–2
Homestead Act, 28–29, 30, 50
House of Representatives, US, 32, 45, 46–47, 48, *49*

"If We Must Die" (McKay), 68
Illinois, 63, 74–75, 77–79, 86, 127, 183
immigrants, 55, 58, 71, 149
impeachment, 51, 198, 200–201
Indian Territory, 24, 26–28, 32–33, 36–38, 40, 107, 116
Indigenous peoples, 19–25, *25*, 28, 30, 36–38, 46–47, 107, 116
influenza pandemic (1918), 160, 189–91, 192
internment camps, 143, 145, 150, 153–55, 156–57

Jackson, A. C., *113*, 113–14, 144–45, 157, 162–63
Jackson, Andrew, 21–22, 24–25
Jackson, Genevieve Elizabeth Tillman, 12
Jewish people, 54–55, 149–50, 160, 201
Jim Crow laws, 14–15, 35–36, 40, 53–54, 59, 70, 106, 113, 115, 124
Johnson, Andrew, 46–47, 51, 197–98
Jones, Richard Lloyd, 125–26, 129, 161
Juneteenth, 196–97

Kansas, 39, 106, 127, 161
Kentucky, 5, 82, 83, 192–93
Ku Klux Klan (KKK), 53–55, 57–59, 80, 82, 168, 191

land runs, 27, 28–30, 32, 38, 41, 104
Lincoln, Abraham, 43–46, 78–79, 196–97
looting, 78–79, 101, 142, 150, 158, 165

Louisiana Purchase, 19–21, 41
Lovecraft Country (HBO), 184
lynchings, 6–10, 16–17, 54,
    60–63, 75, 85, 168, 202
    in Oklahoma, 59, 64–67,
    93–94, 128–29
Macbeth (Shakespeare), 77
Mack, Daniel, 83–84
McCullough, Willard, 94–95, 97,
    100, 136, 138
McKay, Claude, 68
Minnesota, 60–61, 114, 194–95
Mississippi, 24, 48, 82, 83,
    105, 110
Missouri, 1, 3–5, 6–10, 47, 155,
    191–92
mobs, white, 6–9, 57–58, 61,
    92, 128, 200–201. *See also*
    race riots
Mount Zion Baptist Church,
    112–13, 146–47, *147*, 158,
    173, 180
murder allegations, 8, 9, 59–60,
    66, 88, 96, 192
Muscogee (Creek) Nation, 23, 24,
    25, 26–27, 37

National Association for the
    Advancement of Colored
    People (NAACP), 63, 64, 69,
    75–78, *76*, 79–80, 84, 88
National Guard, 75, 98, 136–39,
    145, 150, 153, 155, 185, 200
newspapers, 30, 74, 92, 119, 167.
    See also specific newspapers
New York, 56, 63, 70, 72, 75, *76*,
    80, 111, 120, 121, 162, 193
New York Times, 4, 67, 167, 182,
    195, 197–98
Nida, Homer, 64–65

oil, 30–32, 41, 104–5, 107
Oklahoma, 19–28, *25*, 30–33,
    35–37, 39–40, 111, 113. *See
    also specific cities*
    lynchings in, 59, 64–67,
    93–94, 128–29
Oklahoma Eagle, 175–76

Page, Sarah, 16–17, 60, 164–65
Parrish, Mary Elizabeth Jones,
    140, 150, 157, 168, *168,* 174
Pennsylvania, 55, 191–93
Perryman, Benjamin, 27
Phillips, William "Choc," 101, 139
planes, 110, 141–42, 149
plaques, 10, 176–77
Plessy v. Ferguson, 14–15
police, 17, 55–59, 64–66, 75, 78, 86,
    193–95. *See also* Tulsa Police
postcards, *144, 159,* 167–68
property damage, 78, 141–42,
    146–47, *147,* 157–58, *159,*
    161–64, *164*

race riots, 67, 69, 74–79, 83,
    85–89
    in Tulsa, 65–66, 94–101,
    137–47
racial equality, 45–46, 51, 71,
    79–80, 89, 97, 106, 198
racism, 34–35, 47, 49, 50–53, 58,
    62, 70, 122
    in US Army, 72–73, 82–85
railroads, 28, 31, 34–35, 52, 71,
    106, 123
    Frisco railroad, 104, 108, 117,
    136, 138, *143*
Rainey, Joseph, 48, *49*
Ramsey, Delois Vaden, 102
rape allegations, 6, 16–17, 59–61,
    130
Reconstruction (era), 2, 45–54,
    197
Red Cross, 155–58
reparations, 178–79, 181,
    183–84, 185–86
Republicans, 33–35, 45–48, 125,
    127–28, 198
Revels, Hiram Rhodes, 48, *49*
Richardson, Simon R., 152
rights, 2, 30, 34, 45–47, 80,
    173–74
    voting, 2, 34, 48, 51, 52–53,
    70, 198–99
Roosevelt, Franklin D., 34
Roosevelt, Theodore, 33
Rowland, Dick (Jimmie Jones),
    13–14, 15–17, 60, 97–98,
    129, 138
Russwurm, John B., 120–21

Scott, Julius Warren, 42
segregation, 14–15, 35–36, 40,
    53–54, 86, 106–7, 113–15, 174
Senate, US, 45, *49,* 51, 82,
    199–200
Shakespeare, William, 77
Sinha, Manisha, 197–98
slave patrols, 56–57, 195–96
slavery, 1–3, 22, 36–38, 40–41,
    56, 107, 171. *See also* aboli-
    tion, of slavery
Smith, Beulah Lane Keenan, 18
Smitherman, A. J., 66, 92, 96,
    110, 127–29, 138, 161–63,
    175, 183
Stradford, J. B., 96, 105–7, 114,
    141, 161, 163, 173, *173,* 183
Supreme Court, US, 14–15, 24,
    53, 80, 88, 107, 179
survivors, 118, 141, 148, 150,
    153–58, 161–63, 170–73,
    178–79, 185–87

Taylor, Breonna, 192–93
Taylor, Horace "Peg Leg," 147–48
Tennessee, 22, 47, 53, 62–63, 75,
    76, 113

Texas, 20, 196–97
Trail of Tears, 3, *25,* 25–26, 36, 178
Trump, Donald J., 190–91,
    196–99, 200–201
Tulsa, Oklahoma. *See specific
    topics*
Tulsa Daily World, 124–25
Tulsa Democrat, 123–25
Tulsa Police, 91–92, 94, 97–101,
    116, 130
    during Tulsa Race Massacre,
    142, 145, 162, 164, 179
Tulsa Star, 66, 92, 96, 110,
    127–28, 161–62, 175
Tulsa Tribune, 66, 92–94, 96, 125,
    126, *126,* 129–32, 161, 169
Tulsa World, 66, 92, 130–31, 162,
    165, 186
Turner, Robert, 166

Union army, 44–45, 51, 81
United States (US), 119, 160–62,
    167, 169–70, 189–203, 192–
    96. *See also specific topics*
    federal government, 23, 28,
    34, 54, 122–23
University of Tulsa, 170–71

veterans, 9, 53, 171
    Black, 81–84, 88, 97, 99–100,
    113, 135, 147
    WWI, 83–84, 88, 97, 135,
    146, 147
vigilante justice, 6, 9, 57–60, 64,
    82, 116
voting rights, 2, 34, 47, 51, 52–53,
    70, 198–99

Washington, DC, 43, 72, 85–86,
    121, 184, 199–200
Washington Post, 177, 182,
    197, 199
Watchmen (HBO), 183–84
Wells-Barnett, Ida Bell (aka Ida B.
    Wells), 62–63, *62,* 74, 79, 188
Wheeler, Ed, 172
white men, 84–88, 99–100,
    138–39, 144–45
white people, 89, 99, 137,
    148–49, 156–57, 162, 164,
    165, 170–71, 172
white Tulsans, 115–17, 132–33,
    141, 148–49, 160, 165, 167
white women, 9, 59–61, 67, 77,
    83, 85, 138, 193–95
Williams, Seymour, 136, 146
Williams, W. D. (Bill), 95–96,
    111, 173
Wilson, Woodrow, 54, 71, 190–91
Woolley, James, 65–66, 94
World War I (WWI), 71–74, 81, 85,
    99–100, 142, 191
    veterans, 83–84, 88, 97, 135,
    146, 147